FROM A GIRL'S POINT OF VIEW

LILIAN BELL

From A Girl's Point of View

Lilian Bell

© 1st World Library – Literary Society, 2004
PO Box 2211
Fairfield, IA 52556
www.1stworldlibrary.org
First Edition

LCCN: 2004195338

Softcover ISBN: 1-4218-0169-8
Hardcover ISBN: 1-4218-0069-1
eBook ISBN: 1-4218-0269-4

Purchase *"From A Girl's Point of View"*
as a traditional bound book at:
www.1stWorldLibrary.org/purchase.asp?ISBN=1-4218-0169-8

1st World Library Literary Society is a nonprofit
organization dedicated to promoting literacy by:

- Creating a free internet library accessible from any
computer worldwide.
- Hosting writing competitions and offering book
publishing scholarships.

From A Girl's Point of View
contributed by Tim, Ed & Rodney
in support of
1st World Library Literary Society

Dedicated

WITH MANY APPREHENSIONS TO
THE DULL READER WHO WILL INSIST UPON
TAKING THIS BOOK LITERALLY

CONTENTS

THE UNTRAINED MAN UNDER THIRTY-FIVE

"Since we deserved the name of friends,
And thine effect so lives in me,
A part of mine may live in thee,
And move thee on to noble ends."

Every woman has had, at some time in her life, an experience with man in the raw. In reality, one cannot set down with any degree of accuracy the age when his rawness attacks him, or the time when he has got the last remnant of it out of his system. But a close study of the complaint, and the necessity for pigeon-holing everything and everybody, lead one to declare that somewhere in the vicinity of the age of thirty-five man emerges from his rawness and becomes a part of trained humanity - a humanity composed of men and women trained in the art of living together.

I am impressed with Professor Horton's remarks on this subject: "It has sometimes struck me as very singular," he says, "that while nothing is so common and nothing is so difficult as living with other people, we are seldom instructed in our youth how to do it well. Our knowledge of the subject is acquired by experience, chiefly by failures. And by the time that we have tolerably mastered the delicate art, we are on the point of being called to the isolation of the grave - or shall I say to the vast company of the Majority?

"But an art of so much practical moment deserves a little more consideration. It should not be taught by chance, or in fragments, but duly deployed, expounded, and enforced. It is of far more pressing importance, for example, than the art of playing the piano or the violin, and is quite as difficult to learn.

"It is written, 'It is not good that man should be alone'; but, on the other hand, it is often far from good to be with him. A docile cat is preferable, a mongoose, or even a canary. Indeed, for want of proper instruction, a large number of the human race, as they are known in this damp and foggy island, are 'gey ill to live wi',' and no one would attempt it but for charity and the love of God."

Now who but women are responsible for the training of men? If the mother has neglected her obvious duty in training her son to be a livable portion of humanity, who but the girls must take up her lost opportunities? It is with the class of men whose mothers *have* neglected to train them in the art of living that we have to deal; the man with whom feminine influence - refining, broadening, softening, graciously smoothing out soul-wrinkles, and generously polishing off sharp mental corners - has had no part. It need not necessarily mean men who have not encountered feminine influence, but it does mean those who never have yielded to it. The natural and to-be-looked-for conceit of youth may have been the barrier which prevented their yielding. There is a time when the youth of twenty knows more than any one on earth could teach him, and more than he ever will know again; a time when, no matter how kind his heart, he is incased in a mental haughtiness before which plain Wisdom is dumb. But a time will come when the keenness of some girl's stiletto of wit will prick the empty bubble of his flamboyant egoism, and he will, for the first time, learn that he is but an untrained man under thirty-five.

This elastic classification does not obtain with either geniuses or fools. It deals with the average man as the average girl knows him, and may refer to every man in her acquaintance or only to one. It certainly *must* refer to one! Misery loves company to such an extent that I could not bear to think that there was any girl living who did not occasionally have to grapple with the problem of at least one man in the raw, if only for her own discipline.

You cannot argue with the untrained man under thirty-five. In fact, I never argue with anybody, either man or woman, because women are not reasonable beings and men are too reasonable. I never am willing to follow a chain of reasoning to its logical conclusion, because, if I do, men can make me admit so many things that are not true. I abhor a syllogism. Alas, how often have I picked my cautious way through three-quarters of one, only to sit down at the critical moment, declaring I would not go another step, and then to hear some argumentative man cry, "But you admitted all previous steps. Don't you know that this naturally *must* follow?" Well, perhaps it *does* follow, only I don't believe it is true. It may be very clever of the men to reason, and perhaps I am very stupid not to be able to admit the truth of their conclusions, but I feel like declaring with Josh Billings, "I'd rather not know so much than to know so much that ain't so."

Conversation with the untrained man under thirty-five is equally impossible, because he never converses; he only talks. And your chief accomplishment of being a good listener is entirely thrown away on him, because a mere talker never cares whether you listen or not as long as you do not interrupt him. He only wants the floor and the sound of his own voice. It is the trained man over thirty-five who can converse and who wishes you to respond.

The untrained man desires to be amused. The trained man wishes to amuse. A man under thirty-five is in this world to be made happy. The man over thirty-five tries to make you happy.

There is no use of uttering a protest. You simply must wait, and let life take it out of him. The man under thirty-five is being trained in a thousand ways every day that he lives. Some learn more quickly than others. It depends on the type of man and on the length of time he is willing to remain in the raw.

You can do little to help him, if you are the first girl to take a hand at him. You can but prepare him to be a little more amenable to the next girl. His mind is not on you. It is centred on himself. You are only an entity to him, not an individual. He cares nothing for your likes and dislikes, your cares or hopes or fears. He only wishes you to be pretty and well dressed. Have a mind if you will. He will not know it. Have a heart and a soul. They do not concern him, because he cannot see them. He likes to have you tailor-made. You are a Girl to him. That's all. The eyes of the untrained man under thirty-five are never taken off himself. They are always turned in. He is studying himself first and foremost, and the world at large is interesting to him only inasmuch as it bears relation to himself as the pivotal point. He fully indorses Pope's line, "The proper study of mankind is man," and he is that man. Join in his pursuit if you will; show the wildest enthusiasm in his golf record or how many lumps of sugar he takes in his coffee, and he will evince neither surprise nor gratitude for your interest. You are only showing your good taste.

Try to talk to the untrained man under thirty-five upon any subject except himself. Bait him with different topics of universal interest, and try to persuade him to leave his own point of view long enough to look through the eyes of the world. And then notice the hopeless persistence with which he avoids your dexterous efforts and mentally lies down to worry his Ego again, like a dog with a bone.

The conceit of one of these men is the most colossal specimen of psychological architecture in existence. As a social study, when I have him under the microscope, I can enjoy this. I revel in it, just as I do in a view of the ocean or the heavens at night - anything so vast that I cannot see to the end of it. It suggests eternity or space. But oh! what I have suffered from a mental contact with this phase of him in society! Sometimes he really is ignorant - has no brains at all - and then my suffering is lingering. Sometimes he really knows a great deal - has the making of a man in him, only it lies fallow for want of training - and then my suffering is acute. When success - business or social or athletic or literary or artistic - comes to the untrained man under thirty-five, it comes pitifully near being his ruin. The adulation of the world is more intoxicating and more deadly than to drink absinthe out of a stein; more insidious than opium; more fatal than poison. It unsettles the steadiest brain and feeds the too-ravenous Ego with a food which at first he deemed nectar and ambrosia, but which he soon comes to feel is the staff of life, and no more than he deserves. With success should come the determination, be you man or woman, to fall upon your knees every day and pray Heaven for strength to keep from believing what people tell you, so that you still may be bearable to your friends and livable to your family.

I know that all this will fall unkindly upon the ears of many a worthy man under thirty-five whose charm is still in embryo, and that, unless he is very clever, he will be mortally offended, and never believe my solemn assertion that I am the stanchest friend the man of possibilities has. Let him take care how he resents my amiable brutality, or how he denounces me as his enemy, for if I were not interested in the untrained man under thirty-five I wouldn't bother with him, would I?

I know, too, that a diplomatic feminine contingency will raise a howl of protest, and will read this aloud to men under thirty-five for the express purpose of disclaiming all complicity with such heterodox views, and doubtless will be able to make the men believe them. Tactful girls are a necessity, and I approve of them. I do not in the least mind their disclaiming my views to specific men, especially if I can catch their eye for one subtle moment when the men are not looking. On this subject there is a certain delicately veiled, comprehending, soul-satisfying, mental *wink* going the rounds of the girls, indicating our comrade-ship and unanimity of thought quite as understandingly as the fraternal grip stands for fellowship among masons. We girls have been thinking these things for a long time, and, with this declaration of independence, the shackles will fall from many a girl's soul, because another girl has dared to speak out in meeting.

Of course, I know, too, that girls with nice brothers and cousins and husbands under thirty-five will also offer violent protest. I am perfectly willing. Doubtless their feminine influence has circumvented nature to such an extent that no one would suspect that their men were under thirty-five. I only beg of them to remember that I am not discussing girl-trained men or widowers. Both of these types are as near perfection as a man can become.

A man whom girls have trained is really modest. Even at twenty he does not think that he knows it all. He is willing to admit that his father and mother have brains, and that thirty years' experience entitles them to a hearing. He also is willing to give the girls a show, to humor them, to find them interesting as studies, but never to claim to understand them. In short, he has many of the charming qualities of the man over thirty-five and the widower. That is the man who is girl-trained. But Heaven help the man who is girl-spoiled.

Far be it from me to say that the untrained man under thirty-five, at his worst, is of no use in this world. He is excellent for a two-step. I have used a number of them very successfully in this way. But I know the awful thought has already pierced some people's brains - what if the man under thirty-five does not dance?

Sometimes an untrained man under thirty-five will actually have the audacity to say to me that he takes small pleasure in society because the girls he meets are so silly, and he must use small-talk in order to meet them on their own ground. I am aghast at his temerity, as he, too, will be when he has heard our side of the subject. We girls never have allowed ourselves the luxury of vindicating ourselves, or refuting this charge. It is the clever girl who suffers most of all - not the brilliant, meteoric girl - but just the ordinarily clever girl, as other girls know her. It is this sort of a girl who drags upon my sympathies, because she occupies an anomalous position.

Being a real woman, she likes to be liked. She wishes to please men. We all do. But what kind of men are we to please? Untrained men under thirty-five? Owing to the horrible prevalence of these men, some girls become neither fish nor flesh nor good red herring. They see their silly, pink-cheeked sisters followed and admired. They know either how shallow these girls are or how cleverly hypocritical. Clever girls are also human. They love to go about and wear pretty clothes, and dance, and be admired quite as much as anybody.

The result is that they adopt the only course left to them, and, bringing themselves down to the level of the men, feign a frivolity and a levity which occasionally call forth from a thinking man a criticism which is, in a sense, totally undeserved. What will not the untrained man under thirty-five have to answer for on the Day of Judgment!

It is of no use to argue about this state of things. Facts are facts. Men make no secret of the kind of women they want us to be. We get preached at from pulpits and lectured at from platforms and written about by "The Saunterer" and "The Man About Town" and "The One Who Knows It All," telling us how to be womanly, how to look to please men, how to behave to please men, and how to save our souls to please men,

Lilian Bell

until, if we were not a sweet, amiable set, we would rebel as a sex and declare that we thought we were lovely just the way we were, and that we were not going to change for anybody.

You lords of creation ought to be very complaisant, or else very much ashamed of yourselves. You send in an order: "The kind of girl that I like is a Methodist without bangs." And some nice girl begins to look up Methodist tenets and buys invisible hairpins and side combs. Or you say, "Give me an athletic girl." And, presto! some girl who would much rather read buys a wheel, and learns golf, and lets out the waists to her gowns, and revels in tan and freckles. We do what you men want us to. And, then, when you complain about our lack of brains, that we cannot discuss current events, and that you have to give us society small-talk, I feel like saying: "Well, whose fault is it? If you demand brains, we will cultivate them. If you want good looks, we will try to scare up some. If you want nobility, we will let you know how much we have concealed about us."

Often it is not that we are not secretly much more of women, and better and cleverer women, than you think us. But there is no call for such wares, so we lay character and brain on the shelves to mildew, and fill the show-windows with confectionery and illusion. We supply the demand. We always have supplied it, and we always will.

Of course, some of us get very much disgusted with the débutantes. But, aside from the great superiority they have over girls with thinking powers (in regard to the number of men who admire them, for all men admire cooing girls with dimples) - aside from this, I say, there is something to be said on their behalf. Don't you believe, you dear, unsuspicious men, who dote upon their pliability and the trustfulness of their innocent, limpid blue or brown-eyed gaze, which meets your own with such implied flattery to your superior strength and intelligence - don't you believe for one moment that the simple little dears do not know exactly the part they are playing. They are twice as clever as the cleverest of you. They feel that they are needed just as they are. The fashionable schools are turning them out every year exactly as the untrained men under thirty-five would wish them to be. They know this. Therefore they remain as art has made them. Feeling themselves admired by the class of men they most wish to attract, they have no incentive to improve.

And yet, I suppose, untrained men under thirty-five have their use in the world, aside from the part they play in the discipline of discriminating young women. Girls even marry these men. Lovely girls, too. Clever girls - girls who know a hundred times more than their husbands, and are ten times finer grained. I wonder if they love them, if they are satisfied with them, if *ennui* of the soul is not a bitter thing to bear?

I am always wondering why girls marry them. Every week brings me knowledge that some lovely girl I know has found another man under thirty-five, or that some of my men friends of that persuasion have married out-of-town girls. It does not surprise me so much when girls from another city marry them. Most men do not like to write letters, and visits are only for over Sunday.

Men are always saying, "Well, why don't you tell us

Lilian Bell

the kind of men you would like us to be?" And their attitude when they say it is with their thumbs in the arm-holes of their waistcoats. When a man is thoroughly satisfied with himself he always expands his chest.

There is something very funny to me in that question, because I suppose they really think they would change to please us. I do not mind talking about it, because I am sociable, and I like conversation; but I never for a moment dream that they will do it. They intend to, and their inclination is always to please us, even to spoil us; but they either cannot or will not change; and they think if they can refuse pleasantly, and mentally chuck us under the chin and make us smile, that they have succeeded in getting our minds off a troublesome subject.

Of course, it is partly our fault that we do not insist, but no one wants to be disagreeable. Therefore we choose personal discomfort for ourselves rather than to demand radical changes in the men, which might bring on contention.

But women wish to please men, aside from their power of winning them. Whereas if men can get the girls without any change on their part, they consider themselves a howling success. But they might be a little bit surprised if they could read the minds of these very wives whom they have won, whose life-work often may be only to improve them so that they will make some other woman the kind of a husband they should have made at first, and then to lie down and die.

So let men beware how they criticise us unfavorably, no matter what their ages, for the truth of the matter is that, be we frivolous or serious, vain or sensible, clever or stupid, rich or poor, we are what the American man has made us. We are supremely grateful to him for the most part, for he has literally made us what we are by the sweat of his brow. But let him beware how he cavils at his own handiwork. 'Tis not for the untrained man under thirty-five to complain of us, when now he knows why we are so.

"I'm not denyin' that women are foolish," says George Eliot. "God Almighty made 'em to match the men."

THE PHILOSOPHY OF CLOTHES

"Last night in blue my little love was dressed;
And as she walked the room in maiden grace,
I looked into her fair and smiling face.
And said that blue became my darling best.
But when, this morn, a spotless virgin vest
And robe of white did the blue one displace,
She seemed a pearl-tinged-cloud, and I was -
space!
She filled my soul as cloud-shapes fill the West.

"And so it is that, changing day by day -
Changing her robe, but not her loveliness -
Whether the gown be blue or white or gray,
I deem that one her most becoming dress.
The truth is this: In any robe or way,
I love her just the same, and cannot love her less!"

If you are interested in the spectacle of letting people
paint their own portraits, at the same time entirely
unconscious that they are doing so, ask a number of
women and girls whether they dress to please men or
other women, and then listen carefully to what they say
and watch their faces well while they are saying it.
Most of the girls will say they dress to please women;
and the reason I ask you to watch their faces is that you
may see the subtle changes going on by which they

persuade themselves that they are telling the truth. Women - nice, sweet women, the kind *we* know - seldom tell a real untruth. But they have a way of persuading themselves that what they are about to say is the truth. Women must believe in themselves before they can hope to make other people believe in them; therefore they have themselves to persuade first of all. Now, when men are going to utter an untruth they never care whether they believe it or not, as long as they can make other people believe it. And the so-called brutal honesty of man is only brutal want of tact. That poor, patient, misused word, "honesty"! How sick it must get of its abuse!

Yes, girls really believe, I suppose, that they dress for other girls. But they do not. They dress for men. And only experience will teach them the highest wisdom in the matter. But that they cannot acquire until they believe that only another woman will know just how well they are dressed, and, above all, whether Doucet turned them out, or a dress-maker in the house at two dollars a day.

Men only take in the effect. Women know how the effect is produced. Of course, now I am speaking of the general run of men and women: neither the man who clerked at Cash & Silk's nor the one who pays his wife's bills in Paris, but the man in his native state of charming ignorance of materials; the man who always suggests a "gusset" as a remedy for too scant a gown, who calls insertion "tatting," and who, in setting out for the opera, will tell his wife to put on her "bonnet and shawl," although she may have on point-lace and diamonds. In his more modern aspect he tells you that a girl at the Junior Promenade had on a blue dress with feathers around her neck - which you must translate into meaning anything from blue satin to organdie, and that between dances she wore a feather boa.

It is the effect only that men take in; and when a man goes into ecstasies over a gown of pale green on a hot day just because you look so cool and fresh in it, when you know that you paid but forty cents a yard for it, and only nods when you show him your velvet and ermine wrap, which cost you two hundred dollars, I would just like to ask you if it pays to dress for him. Women know this from a sorrowful experience. Girls have to learn it for themselves. A ball-dress of white tarlatan, made up over white paper cambric, with a white sash, will satisfy a man quite as well as a Paris muslin trimmed with a hundred dollars' worth of Valenciennes lace and made up over silk. Most of them would never know the difference.

I do not know whether to be sorry for these men or not. It must be lovely not to agonize and plan and worry to have everything the best of its kind. I would like to take in only the effect, and never know why I was pleased. Too much analysis is death to unmitigated rapture. You always are haunted by knowing exactly what is lacking, and just how it could be remedied. But these dear men are singularly deluded in many ways, and upon these delusions clever women play, as a master plays upon an organ. And young girls, who have not had time to study into the philosophy of it - how should the poor things know that clothes have any philosophy? - as usual, have to suffer for it.

One of these delusions is the "simple white muslin" delusion. When a man speaks of a "simple white muslin" in the softly admiring tone which he generally adopts to go with it, he means anything on earth in the line of a thin, light stuff which produces in his mind the effect of youth and innocence. A ball-dress or a cotton morning-gown is to him a "simple white muslin."

Now a word with you, you dear, unsophisticated man. I have heard you, with the sound of your hundred-and-fifty-dollar-a-month salary ringing in your ears, gurgle and splash about a girl who wears "simple white muslins" to balls; and I have heard you set down, as extravagant, and too rich for your purse, the girl who wears silk. There is no more extravagant or trouble-some gown in the world than what you call a "simple white muslin." In the first place, it never is muslin, unless it is Paris muslin, which is no joke, if you are thinking of paying for it yourself, as it necessitates a silk lining, which costs more than the outside. If it is trimmed with lace, that would take as much of your salary as the coal for all winter would come to. If trimmed with ribbons, they must be changed often to freshen the gown, whose only beauty is its freshness. Deliver me from a soiled or stringy white party-dress! If it can be worn five times during the winter, the girl is either a careful dancer or else a wallflower. In either case, after every wearing she must have it pressed out and put away as daintily as if it were egg-shells, all of which is the greatest nuisance on earth. Often such a gown is torn all to pieces the first time it is worn. Scores of "simple white muslin" ball-gowns at a hundred dollars apiece are only worn once or twice.

Now take the "extravagant" girl with her flowered taffeta silk, or plain satin, or brocade dress. There is at once the effect of richness and elegance. No matter how sweet and pretty she is, you at once decide that you never could afford to dress her. But that taffeta cost, perhaps, only a dollar a yard. The satin, possibly a dollar and a half. They require almost no trimming, because the material is so handsome and the effect must be as simple as possible. Such a gown never need be lined with silk unless you wish to do it. Many a girl gets up such a gown for fifty or sixty dollars. And then think of the service that there is in it. It does not tear, it does not crush. When she comes home she looks as fresh as when she started. When it soils at the edge of the skirt, she has it cleaned, and there she is with a new dress again. Do you call that extravagant? Why, my dear sirs, it is only the very rich who can afford to wear "simple white muslins!"

There is a hollowness about having a man praise your gowns when you know he doesn't know what he is talking about. When a man praises your clothes he always is praising you in them. You never will hear a man praise even the good dressing of a woman he dislikes; while girls who positively hate another girl often will add, "But she certainly does know how to dress."

And so the experienced woman wears her expensive clothes for other women, and produces her "effects" for men. She wears scarlet on a cold or raw day, and the eyes of the men light up when they see her. It makes her look cheerful and bright and warm. She wears gray when she wants to look demure. Let a man beware of a woman in silvery gray. She looks so quiet and dove-like and gentle that she has disarmed him before she has spoken one word, and he will snuggle down beside her and let her turn his mind and his pocket-book wrong side out. A woman could not look designing in light gray if she tried. He dotes upon the girl in pale blue. Pale blue naturally suggests to his mind the sort of girl who can wear it, which is generally a blonde with soft, fluffy hair, fair skin, and blue eyes - appealing, trustful, baby-blue eyes. Did you ever notice that men always instinctively put confidence in a girl with blue eyes, and have their suspicions of a girl with brilliant black ones, and will you kindly tell me why? Is it that the limpid blue eye, transparent and gentle, suggests all the soft, womanly virtues, and because he thinks he can see through it, clear down into that blue-eyed girl's soul, that she is the kind of girl he fancies she is? I think it is; but some of the greatest little frauds I know are the purry, kitteny girls with big, innocent blue eyes.

Blazing black eyes, and the rich, warm colors which dark-skinned women have to wear, suggest energy and brilliance and no end of intellect. Men look into such eyes and seem not to be able to see below the surface. They have not the pleasure of a long, deep gaze into immeasurable depths. And so they think her designing and clever, and (God save the mark!) even intellectual, when perhaps she has a wealth of love and devotion and heroism stored up behind that impulsive disposition and those dazzling black eyes which would do and dare more in a minute for some man she had set that great heart of hers upon than your cool-blooded, tranquil blonde would do in forty years. A mere question of pigment in the eye has settled many a man's fate in life, and established him with a wife who turned out to be very different from the girl he fondly thought he was getting.

Yet whenever I complain to experienced married women of how discouraging it is to wear your good clothes for unappreciative men, they beg me not to be guilty of the heresy of wishing things different. If they have married one of the noticing kind, they tell me harrowing tales of gorgeous costumes having been cast aside because these critical men made fun of, or were prejudiced against them, and "made remarks." And they point with envy to Mrs. So-and-So, whose husband never knows what she has on, but who thinks she looks lovely in everything, so that she is at liberty to dress as she pleases. When a woman defers to her husband's taste, she sometimes is the best-dressed woman in the room. And sometimes another woman, dressing according to another man's taste, is the worst-dressed. So you see you never can tell. "De mule don't kick 'cordin' to no rule."

There is something rather pathetic to me about a man being so ignorant of why a woman's dress is beautiful, but only the effect remaining in his memory. He remembers how she looked on a certain day in a certain gown. He thinks he remembers her dress. He thinks he would know it again if he saw it. But the truth is that he is remembering the woman herself, her face, her voice, her eyes - above all, what she said, and how she said it. If she wore a scarlet ribbon in her dark hair, a red rose in another woman's hair will most unaccountably bring it all back to him, and he will not know why he suddenly sees the whole picture rise out of the past before his eyes, nor why his throat aches with the memory of it.

I know one of these men, whose descriptions of a woman's dress are one of the experiences of a lifetime. He loves the word bombazine. His mother must have worn a gown of black bombazine during his impressionable age. And he never will be successful in describing a modern gown until bombazines again become the rage. This same dear man brought back to his invalid wife a description of a fashionable noon wedding, which consisted of the single item that the bride wore a blue alpaca bonnet. It really would be of interest from a scientific point of view to know what suggested that combination to any intelligence, even if it were masculine.

I have more evidence to go on, however, when I wonder why the idea of the cost penetrates this same man's brain when shown a new gown by any member of his family, all of whom he is weak enough to adore. His daughter will say, "Papa, do look here just one minute! How do you like my new gown?" And the answer never varies: "Very pretty, indeed. I hope it's paid for." He will say that of a cotton frock made two years ago - he never knows - of a silk *négligé*, or of a ball-gown of the newest make. The fashion produces no impression upon him, nor the material, nor the cut. But let his daughter put on any kind of a pale green dress, and stand before him with the question, "Papa, how do you like my new gown?" While he is raising his head from his book he begins the old formula, "Very pretty. I hope - " Then he stops and says, "I have seen that dress before. Child, you grow to look more like your mother every day of your life." And there is a little break in his voice, and before he goes on reading he takes off his glasses and wipes them, and looks out of the window without seeing anything, and sits very still for a moment. It was the sight of the pale green dress. When he came home from the war his lovely young wife, whom he lost when she was still young and beautiful, came to meet him, holding her baby son in her arms for his father to see, and she had worn a pale green gown.

Why certain kinds of clothes are associated in the

Lilian Bell

public mind with certain kinds of women is to me an amusing mystery. Why are old maids always supposed to wear black silks? And why are they always supposed to be thin? - the old maids, I mean, not the silks. Why are literary women always supposed to be frayed at the edges? And why, if they keep up with the fashions and wear patent-leathers, do people say, in an exasperatingly astonished tone, "Can that woman write books?" Why not, pray? Does a fragment of genius corrupt the aesthetic sense? Is writing a hardening process? Must you wear shabby boots and carry a baggy umbrella just because you can write? Not a bit of it. Little as some of you men may think it, literary women have souls, and a woman with a soul must, of necessity, love laces and ruffled petticoats, and high heels, and rosettes. Otherwise I question her possession of a soul.

WOMAN'S RIGHTS IN LOVE

"She has laughed as softly as if she sighed!
She has counted six and over,
Of a purse well filled and a heart well tried -
Oh, each a worthy lover!
They 'give her time' for her soul must slip
When the world has set the grooving;
She will lie to none with her fair red lip -
But love seeks truer loving.

*   *   *   *   *

"Unless you can muse in a crowd all day
On the absent face that fixed you;
Unless you can love as the angels may,
With the breadth of heaven betwixt you;
Unless you can dream that his faith is fast,
Through behooving and unbehooving;
Unless you can DIE when the dream is past -
Oh, never call it loving!"

In love a woman's first right is to be protected from her
friends while she considers the man whom she contem-
plates loving. The well-meant blundering of vitally
interested friends has spoiled many a promising love
affair, which might have resulted in a marriage so
much above the ordinary that it could be termed

satisfactory even by the most captious.

At no time in a girl's life has she a greater right to work out her own salvation in fear and trembling than during the period known among girls as "making up her mind." If she is the right kind of a girl, honest and delicate minded, it is nerve-racking to be talked about, and sacrilege to be talked to. Then the bloom is on the grape, which a rude touch mars forever.

Yet these kind friends never think of the delicate, touch-me-not influences at work in the girl's soul, or that the instinct to hide her real interest in the man precludes the possibility of her daring to ask to be let alone. So they, in their over-zeal and ambition, either make the path of love so easy and inevitable that all the zest is taken out of it for both (for lovers never want somebody to go ahead and baste the problem for them; they want to blind-stitch it for themselves as they go along), or else, by critical nagging, and balancing the eligibility of one suitor against another, these friends so harass and upset the poor girl that she doesn't know which man she wants, and so turns her back upon all.

In point of fact, when a man is in love, and a girl does not yet know her own mind; when she is weighing out their adaptability, and balancing his love for football against her passion for Browning; during the delicate, tentative period, when the most affectionate solicitude from friends is an irritation, there ought to be a law banishing the interested couple to an island peopled with strangers, who would not discover the delicacy of the situation until it was too late to spoil it.

"Woman's rights." I certainly agree with the men who think that those words have a masculine, assertive, belligerent sound. "Equal suffrage" is much more lady-like, and we are by way of getting all we wish of the men on any subject, under the gentlest title by which it may be called. Strange, how, with strong men, force never avails, but the softest methods are the surest and swiftest. Conscentious

However, equal suffrage, wide as it is, is not all that I wish. It does well enough, but it does not cover the entire ground. I never clamored very much for women to be recognized as the equals of men, either in politics or in love, because, if I had clamored at all, I should have clamored for infinitely more than that. *I* should have clamored for men to recognize us as their superiors, and not for equal rights with themselves, but for more, many more rights than they ever dreamed of possessing. 'Tis not justice I crave, but mercy. 'Tis not equality, but chivalry.

In the whole history of the world, from nineteenth-century Public Opinion clear back to the age of chivalry, men never have been inclined to deal out justice to women. It is their watchword with each other, but with women it always is either injustice or mercy. And in spite of all wrongs and all abuses, I say, Heaven bless the men that this is so. Human nature is more fundamental than customs, and what would become of women if we only got our exact deserts, or had absolute justice dealt to us, either by men or other women or on the Judgment Day?

In these latter days of this progressive, woman's century, however, the most thoughtful men are valiant enough to re-adjust themselves to the idea of woman's development, and allow her equality in progressive thought; at the same time maintaining the old-time chivalry of their attitude towards her. If she asks for justice at the hands of these glorious men, she will get it, and they will uncover in her presence and throw away their cigars while they are dispensing it. Equality to them does not mean either rudeness or insolence. They are always gentlemen.

It requires bravery on their part to take this ground, because the sentiment has not as yet grown popular. But a New Man has been created by the development of the New Woman, and he is the highest type we have.

> "Courtesy wins woman as well
> As valor may, but he that closes both
> Is perfect."

Woman's rights! Why, the very first right we expect is to be treated better than anybody else! Better than men treat each other as a body, and better by the individual man than he treats all other women. I abominate the idea of equality, and to be mentally slapped on the shoulder and told I am "a good fellow." I shrink from the idea of independence and cold, proud isolation with my emancipated sister-women, who struggle into their own coats unassisted and get red in the face putting on their own skates, and hang on to a strap in the street-car, in the proud consciousness that they are independent and the equal of men. I never worry myself when a man is on his knees in front of me, tying the ribbons of my slipper, as to whether he considers me his equal politically or not. It is sufficient satisfaction for me to see him there. If he hadn't wanted to save me the trouble, I suppose he wouldn't have offered. He may even think I am not strong enough for such an arduous duty. *That* would not hurt my feelings either. I have an idea that he likes it better to think that I cannot do anything troublesome for myself than to believe that I could get along perfectly without him. In fact - here's heresy for you, O ye emancipated! - I do not in the least mind being dependent on men - provided the men are nice enough. Let them give us all the so-called rights they want to. I shall never get over wanting to get behind some man if I see a cow. Let them give us a vote, if they will. I shall want at least three men to go with me to the polls - one to hold my purse, one to hold my gloves, and the third to show me how to cast my vote.

If women are serious in wanting to vote in politics, why do they notapply to the body politic the same methods they use with the one man which an all-wise Destiny has committed to their keeping?

If all the women in the world should make up their minds that they wanted to vote worse than anything else on earth - worse even than they want their husbands to go to church with them - and each woman would put on her prettiest clothes, and cuddle up to her own particular man in her softest and most womanish way, when she was begging him to get suffrage for her - why, you all know they would do it. Men would get it for us exactly as they would buy us a pair of horses.

Have you men ever thought about practising for suffrage in politics by giving women suffrage in love? Surely you do not doubt that, should you do this, it would not occur to us to stuff the ballot-boxes, or to put up a ticket with any but honorable candidates for our hands. We do not ask nor wish to indicate who shall run for office. Let the men announce themselves candidates. We would not take the initiative there if it were offered to us for a thousand years. All we ask is to be given plenty of time to canvass the honor of the candidates, thoroughly to understand and investigate the platform (with an eye to how near he will come to sticking to his promises after election), and to be allowed to cast a free and untrammelled vote.

Now, men seem to think that if they allowed woman equal suffrage, the bright white light of our honesty would be too strong a glare for their weak eyes - so long accustomed to darkness - to bear. Um - possibly in politics. Hardly in love.

For myself, I consider absolute honesty most unpleasant. I never knew any really nice, lovable women who were unflinchingly honest. But I have known a few iron-visaged, square-jawed women who were so brutally honest that I have most ingloriously fled at the mention of their approach, and solaced myself with a congenial spirit who is in the habit of skirting delicately around painful truth, and a cozy corner in which to abuse the aforesaid iron-visaged carver of helpless humanity, who loves to draw blood with her truth. Such an one will get a vote in politics long before she gets it in love.

No; men need not fear to give us equal suffrage in love. Our honesty will not be disconcerting. (I would even address a private query, at just this point, to the women, begging that the men will skip it, asking women where in the world we would find ourselves if we were unflinchingly honest with the men who love us?) No one will deny that we would even countenance a certain amount of corruption. We fully agree with those men who tell us weakly questioning women that campaign funds are a necessity. We never have been able to discover just where the money in politics went to, but the expenses of a campaign in our line are more in evidence. I doubt if the most straitlaced Puritan will gainsay me when I declare that bribery from the candidates, in the form of theatres, opera-boxes, flowers, bonbons, and books, would not only be tolerated, but even, in a modest manner, encouraged - having, of course, a keen eye as to the elasticity of the campaign fund. But, of course, just as vulgar bribery, *per se*, only catches the easy and unthinking voter in politics, so, in like manner, would these evidences of generosity only capture the less desirable voter in love. When you men are trying for a woman's vote you need give yourselves no uneasiness. If she is worth having, character wins every time. You don't believe that. That is why you trust to bribery to do it all. And it is also why so many of you get the girl you try for - which is about the richest punishment you could receive.

I adore Hamlet. Not because he was so noble as to give up his life to avenge his father's most foul murder. Not because he was a chivalrous King Arthur, to protect Ophelia's womanly pride from the jeers of a coarse court by openly declaring that he had loved her when he hadn't. Not for any of Shakespeare's reasons for painting him a hero. But for two much more reasonable reasons. One that he said, "I myself am indifferent honest" - oh, the humanity of Hamlet! - and the other that, when under the spell of her beauty and in the tentative, interested stage when he cared for her all but enough to ask her to marry him, he had the wit to discover that she was a fool. Imagine the calamity of Hamlet married to Ophelia! That *would* have been a tragedy. Think of a man clever enough to discover that his idol was made of putty - that his sweetheart was a Rosamond Vincy! Hamlet was a wise man. He withdrew in time. Most men have to be married ten years to discover that they have married an Ophelia or a Rosamond.

It is a trite saying that the whole world is behind a woman urging her to marry. But I find much to interest me in trite sayings. I like to get hold of them, and look them through, and turn them wrong side out, and pull them to pieces to find how much life there is in them. Psychological vivisection is not a subject for the humane society. A trite saying has my sympathy. It generally is stupid and shop-worn, and consequently is banished to polite society and hated by the clever. And only because it possessed a soul of truth and a wonderful vitality has it been kept from dying long ago of a broken heart.

Books could be written of the truth of this particular trite saying. The urging, of course, among people whom we know, is neither vulgar nor intentional. It takes the form of jests, of pseudo-humorous questions if a man sends flowers two or three times. But it takes its worst and most common form in the sudden melting away of the family if the man calls and finds them all together. If a man has no specific intentions towards a girl, and has not determined in his own mind that he wants to marry her; if he is only liking her a great deal, with but an occasional wonder in the depths of his own heart whether this girl is the wife for him; to call upon her casually and see the family scatter, and other callers hastily leave, is enough to scare him to death. And the girl herself has a right to be furiously indignant. When eligible young people are in that tentative stage, it is death to a love to make them self-conscious.

I myself am so afraid of brushing the down from the butterfly wings at this point that, occasionally, when I have been calling, and the girl's possible lover has caught me before I could escape in a natural manner, I have doggedly remained, even knowing that perhaps he wished me well away among the angels, rather than to run the risk of making him conscious that I understood his state of mind. Imagine my feelings of anguish, however, at holding on against my will and against theirs, wanting somebody to help me let go! Much better, I solace myself afterwards, that he should wish me away than to look after my retreating form and wish, in Heaven's name, that I had stayed! Better for the girl, I mean. For my own feelings - but I do not count. I am only giving a girl one of her rights in love. A few judicious obstacles but whet a man's appetite - if he is worth having. And I do not mind being a judicious obstacle once in a while - if I like the girl.

As to how far a girl has a right to encourage a man in love, opinions differ. I once asked a clever literary friend of mine, whose husband is so satisfactory that it is quite a delightful shock to discover it, how far men ought to be encouraged to make love.

"Encourage them all you can, my dear. The best of men require all the encouragement one is capable of giving them."

I pondered over that statement. From her point of view it was, of course, perfectly proper. Married men need all the encouragement they can get to keep them making love to their own wives. But from our stand-point, of being girls - and very nice girls too, some of us, if I do say it myself! - how far have we a right to encourage men to make love to us?

Now I like men; and I like girls. So that I never want anybody to be hurt at this very delicate and dangerous game of love-making. But somebody always *is* getting hurt, and although she never makes any fuss about it, it is generally the girl.

There are two reasons for this. One is that love means twice - yes, twenty, forty - times as much to a girl as to a man; and the second is that we are a believing set of human geese, and we believe a great deal of what you men say, which is wrong of us, and much more of what your pronounced actions over us imply, which is worse. Girls are just the same along the main lines of sentiment and hope and trust and belief in men now as they ever were, and most of this talk about the new woman being different is mere stuff and nonsense.

Now, the men come in right at this point and declare that we ought not to believe so much; that until they have actually proposed marriage, often they themselves do not know their own minds; that a man has a perfect right to withdraw, *à la* Hamlet, if he finds insurmountable flaws in the girl's nature, or, what is oftener the case, somebody whom he likes better; and they intimate pretty strongly that broken hearts, or even slightly damaged affections, are largely our own fault, which, from their standpoint, is true enough, and if we were men we would all say so too.

But, looking at it from our standpoint, does it not seem as if the men had all the rights on their side? And will they be as generous in this as they are in everything else where we are concerned, and view the matter from our point of view, with the sidelights turned on?

In the first place, there is practically the whole world

of women before men from which to choose. Think of that! Thousands of women, and with the additional advantage of the right to make the first advances! How many do *we* have to choose from? We can't roam around the world by ourselves, even to *see* all the desirable men, much less manage to meet and study them. *We* have to wait to be approached even by the meagre few which a gracious Providence casts in our way. If a girl receives three proposals, that, I am told, is a fair average. If she receives ten, she is either an heiress or a belle. If she receives more than ten, she must visit in the West. Think now, reasonably, of the limited opportunities of the most fortunate of us, compared with the limitless opportunities of the least fortunate of you.

Then, too, in order to make ourselves desirable, we are not to be forward or unduly prominent. We are to sit quietly at home and wait to be asked. We are not to take a man's words, uttered under the magnetism of our presence, for truth. We are not to judge by his manner if he does not speak. We are not to flirt with any other man when one man is considering us as a possible wife (although we don't know that he is, and it is dangerous to guess), because he does not like that. It shows, he thinks, a "frivolous nature," or "a desire to attract," or a "tendency to flirt," or, it is "unwomanly," or "unworthy a true woman." There are some other things men say to us if several men are attentive at the same time, but I have forgotten the rest. They are very convincing, however. Then, when the man has made up his mind that he wants us as his wife (that grammar sounds polygamous, but my whole philosophy of life is against that idea), why, we are to be ready to drop into his arms like a ripe plum and not keep him on tenter-hooks of anxiety, because only coquettes do that.

Now I am not endeavoring to do an exceptional man justice, who will resent that somewhat broad platform. I am only presenting the attitude of man in general, from a girl's standpoint. And if you will view it as referring to "other men" and not to yourself, you will be quite willing to admit that it is, in the main, true.

Now if, in order to avoid heartaches, and so be able to blame you for something you never intended and which you are not willing to shoulder, we are not to let ourselves go, when we feel like falling in love with you, do you give us leave to allow every one of you to get clear up to the proposing-point and come flatly out with the words "Will you marry me?" before we let you know whether we want you or not, or before we begin to let ourselves go?

Come now. Own up, you men. How well do we girls know you when you have called on us three hundred and sixty-five times in succession? Not at all. We know only what we can see and hear. How well do we know you when we have been engaged to you six months? Not at all. We know only what you have been unable to conceal of your faults, and the virtues you have displayed in your show-windows. How long must a woman be married to a man before she understands him thoroughly - as thoroughly as she ought to have understood him before she ever dared to stand up at an altar and promise to love him and live with him until death did them part?

A broken engagement ought to be considered a blessed thing as a preventive of further and worse ills. But it is not. It militates seriously against a girl. Not so much with men as with women. That is one of the times, and there are many others, when men are broader and more just than women. The ordinary man, taken at random, will say, "Probably he was a worthless fellow." The ordinary woman will say, "She ought to have known her own mind better."

The odd part of all this is that, even if you men, as a body, should say to all the girls: "Go ahead. Encourage us to the top of your bent. Let us propose without any knowledge based on your past actions or words as to whether we are going to be accepted or not, and we will take the result cheerfully and won't rage or howl about it" - that not one of us would do it.

"How conscience doth make cowards of us all!" We might consider that you were only giving us our rights in love. We might theorize beautifully about it, and even vow we were going to take you at your word and do it. But we couldn't. It simply isn't in us. We could not be so unjust to you - so untrue to ourselves. The great maternal heart of woman, which bears the greater part of all the sufferings in this world that the men and little children may go free, prevents us from taking any such so-called rights from you, at the cost of suffering on your part. Women have tenderer hearts than men for a purpose, and if they are hurt oftener than men's, why, that is for us to bear. We cannot make ourselves over and turn Amazons at your expense.

MEN AS LOVERS

"God measures souls by their capacity
For entertaining his best angel, Love."

     *   *   *   *   *

"It is a common fate - a woman's lot -
To waste on one the riches of her soul,
Who takes the wealth she gives him, but cannot
Repay the interest, and much less the whole.

"Are you not kind? Ah, yes, so very kind.
So thoughtful of my comfort, and so true.
Yes, yes, dear heart, but I, not being blind.
Know that I am not loved as I love you.

"One tenderer word, a little longer kiss,
Would fill my soul with music and with song;
And if you seem abstracted, or I miss
The heart-tone from your voice, my world goes
wrong."

Men seldom make perfect lovers. I deeply regret being
obliged to say this, as they are about all we girls have
to depend upon in that line; but it is the solemn truth. I
do not pretend to say why this is so. I suppose it is
because a man never dwells upon the sentimental side

of life, nor understands the emotions, unless he is either a poet or a Miss Nancy, and it is almost equally dangerous to marry either of those.

Pray, do not be offended, my friends the poets, at being mentioned in the same paragraph with a Miss Nancy, until you discover the exact meaning of that effective term of opprobrium. A Miss Nancy is a poet without genius, one who has a talent for discovering the fineness of life, but who lacks the wit to keep his views from ridicule. It is not a step of the seven-league boots between the sublime and the ridiculous. Sometimes it is only an invisible step of the tiniest patent-leathers.

I never could understand why a man who plays a good game of whist should not know how to make love. There are so many points in common. You can play a game of whist with only enough skill to keep your partner's hands from your throat, or you can play it for all there is in it.

Now I am not a whist-player. Ask those who have played with me, and see the well-bred murder in their eyes as they remember their wrongs. They will tell you that I can take all the tricks - not just the odd, but three, four, and five tricks - yet I am not playing whist. I am just winning the game, that is all. If my partner, in an unthinking moment, says, "Let's win this game," we win it. But it is like saying to the cab-driver, "You make that train." We make the train and say nothing about taking off a wheel or two in the process. Once, after a game of this kind, my partner said to me, "Allow me to congratulate you upon a most brilliant game - of cards!"

Now you must not think me either stupid or

blundering. I play with magnificent effrontery, often rushing in where angels fear to tread; but, somehow, effrontery is not the best qualification for a whist-player. I am too lucky at holding the cards, and play each one to win. I am lavish with trumps. I delight to lead them first hand round, but I have not the courage of my convictions, for I always feel little quivers of fear when I do it, because when my trumps and aces are gone, then I'm gone too. I have no skill in finesse, in the subtlety, the delicate moves which are the inherent qualities of a game of whist. To tell the brutal truth, I play my own hand. Could anything be worse, dear shade of Sarah Battle, even if I do win? In short, my manner of playing whist is the way some men, most men, make love.

Now you know, brothers - I call you brothers to prove how very friendly my feelings are towards you, even if I do show you up from our side - you know that a good whist-player is only slightly interested in the play of the great cards. His fine instinct comes into play when the delicate points of the game are in evidence; when it is a question of who holds the seven of clubs, if he leads the six in the last hand, or of the lurking-place of the thirteenth trump. I never can remember anything below the jack, and I give up playing whist forever at least once every month. But I am so weak that I return to it again and again, as a smoker does to his brier-wood. I feel partly vexed and partly sorry for myself when I realize that I cannot play - I can only win. I have seen men win very superior girls, but they have done it in a manner which would disgust a good whist-player. Yet they, too, keep on with their indifferent love-making with the same fatal human weakness which sees me brave the baleful light in my partner's eyes night after night - when I am in a whist-playing community. Many men make love because the girl is convenient and they happen to think about it. It never would occur to me to hunt up three people at a country-house and ask them to play whist. But if three are at a table, and there is no one else, I drop into the vacant place, which could be filled much better by a skilled player, with pathetic willingness.

I wonder if a man ever deliberately made up his mind to marry, and then hunted up his ideal girl? Alas, alas, if he did, I never heard of him! But I have seen scores of them drop into vacant chairs at the girls' sides, and make love just because they were handy.

We hate this "handy" love-making, we girls. You needn't think we don't know it when we hear it. Sometimes we are not so stupid as we pretend. But we never let you see that we are clever enough to understand you, because you don't want us to. And I must say that I cannot blame you. If we girls are pretending to you that we have been waiting all our lives for just you, we dislike to have you discover that we have employed those years of waiting very satisfactorily to ourselves, so much so that a casual observer would not have suspected the emptiness of them.

So your funny little pretences are all very well, provided you do not let us catch you in them. Only - possibly you do not know how many times we do catch you. That is one of the chief points. You never know how many times we see through you and beyond, and know just why you did certain things much better than you yourselves know it. Of course, it would not be wise for us to tell you this individually, for that would break up the meeting; but there is no harm in letting you know in bulk.

I suppose there is not a man in the world who would not be surprised if he knew that we do not consider men good lovers. We have accepted them, and been engaged to them, and married them, and pretended to them, and, what is worse still, pretended to ourselves that they were satisfactory, but the truth is they were not, and they are not, and this is the first time we have dared to say so.

Now don't expect, if you go to your wife or your sweetheart and ask her if this is so, that she is going to tell you the truth about it. I wouldn't either. I would pretend that' the others might be unsatisfactory as lovers, but that you - well, you just suited me, that's all. I would have to, you understand, to keep you going. And that is what your sweetheart will do. If she did not, you would get cross and sulky, and there would be a week of unhappiness for both of you, and then the girl would apologize and back down from her position, and then you would go on exactly as you did before.

No, if you are going to profit by this at all, do not talk it over with any woman you love. Talk it over with some clever woman who will tell you the truth because she has nothing to lose. A man will always take more from a woman whom he does not love than he will from his own sweetheart or wife.

I wonder why things are so. Is it that ideal love is only founded upon the truth and the superstructure is built of fabrications? Is it that we women are much more artistic and more clever at masquerading the truth that we make so much better lovers than the men? Oh, the scores and scores of men who have told me what their wives thought of them, and then the looks these wives have shot at me across the flowers on the dinner-table!

Only one glance, which no man caught, telegraphing, "Do I, though? You are a woman and you know. You know what I would have if I could, but how I have had to make him believe that he was all of that, because he is my husband." Not that she is dissatisfied with him. Not that she would give him up. Not that she would leave him or have anybody else if she could. She loves him all she can, and he loves her all he wants to. He has won the game, but he has not played for all there was in it.

I never have been able to make up my mind whether ideal love was the best, or if love with a great deal of common-sense in it was not the most philosophical and better in the long-run. But to those of us who are romantic it is fearful to think of deliberately turning our backs on terrapin and lobster and ice-cream, and meditating upon plain bread and cold potatoes. You men do not recognize the romantic streak which, of more or less breadth and thickness, runs through every woman, making her love good love-making. You are so terribly practical and common-sense and every-day. We girls like flowers, and mental indigestibles, and occasional Sundays. We do not know why we do, but we do, and we cannot help it, and if you are going to make love according to Hoyle you must recognize this fact, and pamper us in our folly. Don't we pamper you?

Now I know perfectly well how some of you are going to work at it. You will begin by thinking, "Yes, that's true. I've got a girl like that, and, by Jove, I'll humor her!" Bless your dear hearts! Your intentions are always of the best. If only you knew how to carry them out! But the first time you come across a little unreasonable, sentimental folly of hers, you will take her hand in yours and say, "Yes, dear, I understand just what you mean. I know exactly how you feel on the subject, and I am perfectly willing to do what you want me to. But, don't you see, if I do, it would look just a little queer to mother" - (or the boys, or the other fellows, or to Jessie and the girls, or to - you may insert the name for yourself) - "and, while I want to please you, I hardly think that is quite the way to go about it; so, if you will be the dear, sensible little woman that you always are, we will simply take a nice little walk, instead of going to Europe, and I will try to make it just as enjoyable to you. You know I shall be with you, darling, and haven't you often said that you were perfectly happy wherever I was?" And darling will begin a weak argument in favor of her little unreasonable, sentimental whim represented by "Europe," although she sees that your mind is made up. But you have seen her weaken at your smooth talk, and you give her some more; and if that doesn't do, why, you kiss her, and then she's gone. And before you leave her she has assured you that she really would "just as soon" or "much rather" take a walk than go to Europe; and you come out whistling and thinking what a dear little thing she is, and how much you love her. Oh, you have won! Nobody denies that; but look at your partners face if you want to know how you have done it.

Why didn't you do as you said you were going to? Why didn't you do it her way? Why don't you study your sweetheart, and learn to know her, and to know the real woman - the side she never shows to you nowadays Because, just as soon as she sees your way of doing, she is going to hunt up a new way of managing you. It is all your own fault that you are managed (as you all know you are), and your fault that you get pale-gray truth instead of the pure white. It starts out pure white, but it is doctored before it reaches you.

You never are satisfied to do anything else in the slovenly way in which you make love. I know a man who is just an ordinary man in everything else; but to see him drive a spirited horse is to know that he has the making of a good lover in him. He is full of enthusiasm in studying his horse's disposition. He will interrupt the most interesting conversation to say, "There, Pet, that pile of stones won't hurt you. Go on, now, like the pretty little lady that you are. Here's a nice bit of road. Hold your head up and just show what you can do. That's right. That's my beauty. See how she reaches out. Isn't she handsome? Quiet, now, Pet. Take this hill easily. We know you could keep up that pace for an hour, but you mustn't tire yourself all out just because you have a willing spirit. See her look around to see if I am pleased with her!" "Dear me, that's nothing," I said. "Any woman would do as much, if you treated her that way." He is responsive, so he grinned appreciatively. He spends hours studying that horse's traits. He is always saying that she won't back, or that she hates this and is afraid of that. His horse, never has to do anything that she doesn't want to; but his wife does.

You men would not do business, or even play golf, without many times the thought you put into your love-making. Of course, now, I am not talking of the sleepless nights or the anxious days you spent before you knew whether she loved you. No, indeed; you did enough thinking and worrying then to please anybody. But I am referring to the girl to whom you are engaged, perhaps you are married to her, and have been for forty years. You are not too old yet to know that you have not been a perfect lover. I know that old story, that men are so fond of telling just here, about a man running for a car before he has caught it. Yes, we know all that. But we want you to keep on running.

However, on the other hand, I know that ideal love is a difficult thing to manage, from our point of view. It is a fearful strain to live up to it. In fact, nobody can do it. But I never could see why you had to stick to one or the other. Why can't you mix the two?

Ideal love is a beautiful thing to think about or to live in for a few weeks or months - according to your temperament. It cannot be equalled for the first part of an engagement or the honeymoon. But it is like going to the theatre and seeing the grandeur of the old gray castle, and the perpetual moonlight, and the devoted love of the satin duchess for the velvet duke. You know that it is just acting, and that the villain is not really going to swim the moat with his band of steel warriors, and burn the castle, and capture the duchess and marry her by force. Yet I love to pretend. I dearly love to take two pocket-handkerchiefs with me and sop them both - and I would like to cry out loud, only I never do; but I always have to pull my veil down and feel my way out of the theatre. I love to throw myself into it, and it always annoys me when the acting is so bad that I cannot. If any man sees any moral in that, let him heed it, and believe that I am only one of ten thousand other girls who would like to throw ourselves into the illusion of it only your acting is so bad that we cannot.

If men would only realize that the material side is what we girls care the least for. Pray do not think, just because you have built us Colonial houses, and have our clothes made for us, and never allow butchers' bills to annoy us, that you have done your whole duty by us. It never occurs to most of us who have those dear American men for husbands and lovers that we ever really could become cold or hungry. You would be very unhappy if you thought anybody belonging to you did not have all the clothes she wanted, and the best in the market. But you think it is a huge joke when we say that we are mentally cold and hungry a great deal of the time, and that you are a storehouse, with all that we need right within your hearts and brains, only you will not give it to us.

When you want to surprise us with a present, what do you do? You buy us a sealskin or a diamond-ring. Is *that* what you think we want? Perhaps some of you have a wife who only wants such things, and who cares for nothing else so much. If so, give them to her. If her higher nature is satisfied with plush, let her have it. Smother her in sealskins, weigh her down to earth with jewels. But the rest of us? What are you going to give us?

LOVE-MAKING AS A FINE ART

"If thou must love me, let it be for naught
Except for love's sake only. Do not say
'I love her for her smile - her look - her way
Of speaking gently - for a trick of thought
That falls in well with mine, and certes brought
A sense of pleasant ease on such a day.'
For these things, in themselves, beloved, may
Be changed or change for thee - and love so wrought
May be unwrought so. Neither love me for
Thine own dear pity's wiping my cheeks dry;
A creature might forget to weep, who bore
Thy comfort long, and lose thy love thereby.
But love me for love's sake, that evermore
Thou mayst love on through love's eternity"

Of course, to begin with, every man honestly believes that he has made, is making, or could make a good lover.

So I admit at the outset that I am talking to the lover who not only is successful in his own estimation, but the one who has been encouraged in that belief by his own sweetheart or wife until he has every right to believe in himself.

You are about to be told the honest truth for once in your life, so much so that your wives and sweethearts will tell me behind your back that every word of it is true. But after you have clamored for years to know "how women honestly felt on such subjects," and when, nettled at not getting the truth from us individually, you have declared that "the best of women are naturally a little bit hypocritical," the loveliest part of it all is that you will not believe a word of what I have said, and, in accordance with that belief, will calmly announce that I don't know what I am talking about.

Well, perhaps I don't. A woman's aim is never quite true. I could not hit the bull's-eye. But in this case, please to remember that I am firing at a barn-door with bird-shot.

I don't blame you for not believing me. It is against your whole theory of life. Not to believe in yourself were a great calamity. My grandfather was so unfortunately accurate that with advancing years he came whimsically to consider himself infallible. And when, urged by the clamoring of his equally accurate family, he sometimes consented o consult the dictionary, and he found that he differed from it, it never disturbed his belief in himself. He closed the book, saying, placidly, "But the dictionary is wrong." He considered such a trifle not worth even getting heated about. He dismissed it with a wave of his hand. But there was a twinkle in his eye. A typical man, you see, was my grandfather. And, in consequence, a great many other people besides himself believed in him.

But to return. Know, first of all, that you cannot cover me with confusion by pointing to your wives to prove that you have been successful lovers. I never said you could not get married. There is nothing intricate about that. Anybody can marry.

Nor am I to be daunted by the fact that you have been so good a lover as to make your wife happy. You may not be considered a perfect lover even if you have compassed that very laudable end. In fact, the very ones I mean are the apparently successful lovers with happy or contented wives.

No shadow of a doubt as to your success as lovers has ever crossed your dear old satisfied minds. To you I am alluding - to the very ones who never gave the subject a thought before. Wake up, now, and listen. Your wives have thought about it enough, even if you have not.

Remember then that I am only trying to tell you, not *why* men fail as lovers, but *how* they fail - in how much you fail.

Leave out all flirting, all precarious engagements, all unhappy Carriages, and presuppose a sweet, lovable woman, contentedly married to a real man - a man who truly loves, even if he has not completely mastered the gentle art of love-making. No skeleton in the closet; no wishing the marriage undone; with no eternal fitnesses of things to make the gods envious; no great joys of having met each other's star-soul; with plenty of little every-day rubs, either in the shape of hateful little economies in the choice of opera-seats and cab-hire, or petty illnesses and nerves. Just a nice, ordinary, pleasant marriage, with only love to keep the machinery from squeaking, and no moral obligation on the man's part to see that the supply of love does not run short. A great many men can stand a squeak constantly. But women have nerves, and will go to any trouble to remove one which their husbands never hear.

You have worked early and late to buy your wife even more luxuries than you really could afford. But you love her so much that it was your greatest pleasure to heap good things upon her. And very nice of you it is. You are a dear, good man to do it, and I honor you for it. Her physical needs are abundantly supplied. Indeed, you are so good a lover that you remember your courting-days enough to send her flowers on her birthdays and Easter. So her sentimental needs, represented by flowers, are supplied.

There remain but two needs more. Those of her mind and heart.

It is too delicate a subject to discuss whether you are clever enough for her. Very likely you are. If not, she ought to have attended to that before she married you, because that is one of the few things that you really can know something about during an engagement - if you are not too much in love to have any sense left at all. Therefore again I take for granted that you and she are congenial. If she is devotedly fond of music, you do not hate it so that you cannot occasionally go with her in the evening to the opera, with abundant props in the shape of tickets for the matinée, to which you generously bid her to "take one of the girls." If she loves books, you like to hear her talk about them, because she does it so well, and because she knows the ins and outs of your mind so thoroughly that in ten minutes she can give you the plot, and half an hour's reading aloud of striking passages will give you so excellent an idea of the style that you can talk about it to-morrow more intelligently than some bachelors who have really read it by themselves most conscientiously. That is because you are clever; because your wife is more clever. You have a brain, and your wife photographs her personality and her subject upon it, because she understands you and has studied you, and has a pride that you shall appear to advantage among her friends and not degenerate into a mere business machine, as too many men do. I suppose it never occurred to you to try to do a similar thing for her. You could, if you wanted to. But it is a good deal of trouble, and you are generally tired. But what do you suppose would happen if you should exhibit the same eagerness that she does to keep the flame of love alive, so that your marriage should not sink to the dead common-place level of all the other marriages you know? Suppose, even after you have caught the car, that you occasionally got off and ran beside it a while, just for healthful exercise, and to keep yourself from growing ordinary?

Suppose *you* occasionally hunted out a new book, and marked it, and brought it home to read to her, not because you think she wouldn't have got it without you, but just to show her that you are trying to pull evenly, and that you wanted to do something extra charming for her *in her line*, and to prove that you have a conscience about keeping this precious, evanescent, but carelessly treated love at a point where it is still a joy. It is a sad thing to get so used to a beautiful exception like love that you never think of it as marvellous.

A man never seems to be able to understand that, in order to obtain the supremest pleasure from an act of thoughtfulness to his wife, he must be wholly unselfish and give it to her, in her line, and the way she wants it - and the way he knows she wants it, if he would only stop to think. I know a man who hates to go out in the evening, but who occasionally, in order to do something particularly sweet and unselfish to please his wife, takes her to the theatre. She loves fine plays, tragedy, high-grade comedy. But he takes her to the minstrels, because that is the only thing he can stand, and for two weeks afterwards he keeps saying to her, "Didn't I take you to the theatre the other night, honey? Don't I sometimes sacrifice myself for your pleasure?" And she goes and kisses him and says yes, and tries not to think that his selfishness more than outweighs his unselfishness. Women have more conscience about deceiving themselves into staying in love than men have.

But even yet, suppose you are not that kind of a man, we have not got to the point of the subject yet. Our way lies through the head to the heart. And the man who is scrupulously careful about acts has yet to. watch at once the greatest joy, the greatest grief, the supremest healing of even deliberate wounds - words. It is a question with me whether a woman ever knows all the joys of love-making who has one of those dumb, silent husbands, who doubtless adores her, but is unable to express it only in deeds. It requires an act of the will to remember that his getting down-town at seven o'clock every morning is all done for you, when he has not been able to tell you in words that he loves you. It is hard to keep thinking that he looked at you last night as if he thought you were pretty, when he did not say so. It is hard to receive a telegram, when you are looking for a letter, saying, "Have not had time to write. Shall be home Sunday. Will bring you something nice." It is harder still to get a letter telling about the weather 'and how busy he is, when the same amount of space, saying that he got to thinking about you yesterday when he saw a girl on the street who looked like you, only she didn't carry herself so well as you do, and that he was a lucky man to have got you when so many other men wanted you, and he loved you, good-bye - would have fairly made your heart turn over with joy and made you kiss the hurried lines and thrust the letter in your belt, where you could crackle it now and then just to make sure it was there.

Nearly all nice men make good lovers in deeds. Many fail in the handling of words. Few, indeed, combine the two and make perfect lovers.

But the last test of all, and, to my mind, the greatest, is in the use of words as a balm. Few people, be they men or women, be they lovers, married, or only friends, can help occasionally hurting each other's feelings. Accidents are continually happening even when people are good-tempered. And for quick or evil-tempered ones there is but one remedy - the handsome, honest apology. The most perfect lover is the one who best understands how and when to apologize.

I have heard men say, to prove their independence, their proud spirit, their unbending self-respect, "I never apologize." They say it in such conscious pride, and so honestly expect me to admire them, and I am so amiable, that I never dare remonstrate. I simply keep out of their way. But I feel like saying: "Poor, pitiful soul! Poor, meagre nature! Not to know the gladness of restoring a smile to a face from which you have driven it. Only to know the coldness of a misnamed pride; never to know the close, warm joy of humility."

Many people know nothing about a real apology. A lukewarm apology is more insulting than the insult. A handsome apology is the handsomest thing in the world - and the manliest and the womanliest. An apology, like chivalry, is sexless. Perhaps because it is a natural virtue of women, it sits manlier upon men than upon women.

... "It becomes
The throned monarch better than his crown."

Even as chivalry, being a natural attribute of men, becomes beautiful beyond words to express when found in women.

I have often heard men say they never apologize. Sometimes I have heard women. Pitiful, indeed, it becomes then. A woman without religion is no more repulsive to me than one who "never apologizes." How I pity the people who love those men and women who "never apologize." A delicate apology brings into play all the virtues necessary to a perfect humanity. The proudest are generally those who can bend the lowest. It is not pride; it is a stupid vanity and an abnormal self-love which prevent a man or woman from apologizing. An apology requires a native humility of which only great souls are capable. It requires generosity to be willing to humble yourself. It takes faith in humanity to think that your apology will be accepted. You must have a sense of justice to believe that you owe it. It requires sincerity to make it sound honest, and tact to do it at the right time. It requires patience to stick to it until the wound has ceased to bleed, and the best, highest, truest type of love to make you want to do it.

There is only one thing meaner than a person who never apologizes, and that is a person who will not accept one.

It requires a finer type of generosity to receive generously than to give generously. And a nature is more divine which can forgive honestly and quickly than one which can only apologize and is not capable of a swift forgiveness. But it is a wise dispensation of Providence that the two are twin virtues, and are generally to be met with in the same broad and beautiful nature.

Used against a high soul, there is no surer method of humiliation than an apology. In one skilled at reading human nature, an apology becomes a weapon. When you are not the one who should apologize first, when you are less to blame than he, be you the one to apologize first, and see how quickly his noble nature will abase itself, and rush to meet you, and how sure and glorious and complete the reconciliation will be!

I never can blame people who refuse to accept an apology in the shape of flowers when the wound has been given in words. The whole of Europe would not compensate some women for a hurt, when the hurt had been distinctly worded and the apology came in the shape of a dumb, voiceless present.

From the standpoint of observation and inexperience, I would say that the supremest lack of men as lovers is the inability to say, "I am sorry, dear; forgive me." And to keep on saying it until the hurt is entirely gone. You gave her the deep wound. Be manly enough to stay by it until it has healed. Men will go to any trouble, any expense, any personal inconvenience, to heal it without the simple use of those simple words. A man thinks if a woman begins to smile at him again after a hurt, for which he has not yet apologized, has commenced to grow dull, that the worst is over, and that, if he keeps away from the dangerous subject, he has done his duty. Besides, hasn't he given her a piano to pay for it? But that same man would call another man a brute who insisted upon healing up a finger with the splinter still in it, so that an accidental pressure would always cause pain.

If you do not believe this, what do you suppose the result would be if you should apologize to your wife for something you said last year. If you think she has forgotten, because she never speaks of it, just try it once.

I honestly believe that the simple phrase, "I am sorry, dear; forgive me," has done more to hold brothers in the home, to endear sisters to each other, to comfort mothers and fathers, to tie friends together, to placate lovers; that more marriages have taken place because of them, and more have held together on account of them; that more love of all kinds has been engendered by them than by any other words in the English language.

GIRLS AND OTHER GIRLS

"Thou art so very sweet and fair,
With such a heaven in thine eyes,
It almost seems an over-care
To ask thee to be good or wise.

"As if a little bird were blamed
Because its song unthinking flows;
As if a rose should be ashamed
Of being nothing but a rose."

* * * * *

* * * * *

"It is so hard for Shrewdness to admit
Folly means no harm when she calls black white."

People who criticise the grammar of those young girls who say "I don't think," should have a care. For it is more true than incorrect. Most girls don't think.

But there are two kinds of girls - girls under twenty-five and others.

Of course, although you may not know it, age has no more to do with that statement than it had to do with the one when I hinted that man reached the ripe state of perfection at the mystic age of thirty-five. These are but approximate figures, and are only for use in general practice. They have no bearing on specific cases, when it is always best to call in a specialist.

I know many girls who are still seeing and hearing unintelligently, and have not begun to assimilate knowledge, even at twenty-five. I know others of twenty, who have assimilated so well that they will never be under twenty-five. But it is a literal fact, and this statement I am willing to live up to, that the majority of girls must have lived through their first youth before a thinking person can take any comfort with them.

I am sure Samuel Johnson had this in mind when he said: "'Tis a terrible thing that we cannot wish young ladies well without wishing them to become old women." Or possibly the exclamation was wrung from him after an attempt to talk to one of them. Many brave men, who would stop a runaway horse, or who would dare to look for burglars under the bed, quail utterly before the prospect of talking to a young girl who frankly says, "I don't think."

How can those girls, who give evidence of no more thought than is evinced by their namby-pamby chatter, call their existence living? They mistake pertness for wit; audacity for cleverness; disrespect to old age for independence; and general bad manners for individuality. Has nobody ever trained these girls to think? What kind of schools do they attend? Who has spoiled them by flattery, until they are little peacocks to whom a mirror is an irresistible temptation?

Why do unthinking parents supply them with money, and never ask how they spend it? How does it come that if you want to find great numbers of them together you go to Huyler's instead of to Brentano's? What kind of women will these girls make, to whom a wrinkle in their waist is of more moment than their soul's salvation?

I often wonder what kind of mothers these girls have. Surely there can be no family conversation where they live. Surely they never hear the great questions of the day discussed at the dinner-table. From the number of hours they spend upon the street, I often am tempted to say, what the poor, tired woman, who stood for miles in the street-car, said to her fellow-passengers, "Have none of yez *homes*?"

Poor, empty-pated little creatures! Poor lovely little clothes-racks, who occasionally organize a concert for newsboys whose lives are busier and more useful than their own! A Street Waifs' Benefit for Street Waifs!

If the crude young person who stands with such eager feet where the brook and river meet that she has wetted her pretty shoon in her haste to be in the society of men could only have the wit to sing:

"O wad some power the giftie gie us,
To see oursels as others see us,"

she might discover strange points of resemblance between herself and a very young baby.

In the earliest days of earthly existence a baby is in a jelly-fish state, from which no one can say what he will emerge. His brain is a sponge. He receives everything and gives nothing. He is pretty to look at, and seems made for nothing but love. He coos and gurgles, he seldom does anything more intelligent than to smile, and he prefers men to women.

The greatest fault that thinking men find with this sort of girl is, that she becomes sillier every day that she lives. I have heard women complain of the degeneracy of the boys who seek their daughters in marriage; but when I look at the many girls of this type I am tempted to say, "Well, madam, who but a degenerate would care to marry your daughter?"

Men claim that it is difficult to maintain their ideals in regard to women, in the face of such selfishness, crudeness, bad manners, and jealousies as exist between young girls of this sort. Of course, they who have become belles by reason of their lovely faces never know that the thinking class of young men criticise them adversely, and they would not care if they did. There are still many men who do admire and who will fall in love with them, and the others are not missed.

We must not blame them too severely for rejoicing in their loveliness. It might be a hard struggle for the rest of us not to do the same if we had their beauty.

Men often wonder why girls' friendships are so hollow. They wonder why we are so ungenerous to each other. "So hateful," *we* call it. Hateful is not a man's word. It is a woman's; and trust a woman to know exactly what it means.

Well, the truth of it is that men are at the bottom of a great deal of it. Girls seldom quarrel with each other except over some man, and, while they intend to be loyal to each other, they cannot seem to manage it if there is a man in the case.

Most girls have two natures. One she shows to men; the other to other girls. What we know of one is the way she droops and is so openly bored by other girls that it is quite a blow to our vanity to be obliged to be with her. We recognize the other at the approach of a man, even if we cannot see him, by the changes in the girl's face. She straightens herself, puts a hand on each side of her waist, and pushes her belt down lower, moistens her lips, a sparkle comes into her eyes, she touches her back hair, and runs a finger under the edge of her veil. Then she smiles - such a smile as the other girls have not been able to win from her in three hours.

These girls are very clever sometimes - even these little, soft, kitteny girls, who do not know anything about books, who never read, who never study, and are popularly called empty-headed even by the very men who make love to them. These girls are keen beyond words to express in their intuitive knowledge of human nature and the differentiation between man nature and woman nature. They are capable of using the outward and apparent motives of humanity for an effect, and secretly of plying the subtlest and most occult.

It is difficult to designate their exact methods, and dangerous to exploit them, for you immediately lay yourself open to the suspicion of being capable of the same double-dealing yourself, or of its being beneath your dignity to accuse any one of such duplicity; and yet there are the causes and there are the results. You can shut your eyes to them if you wish.

It is just here where a girl of this kind is so uncanny. Of course, for those of us who wish to take a lofty view of love and lovers, who wish to think each woman sought out by a man for her beauty and virtues and married for love, it is very repugnant to have to face the fact that there are hundreds of sweet, nice girls, of good family and good training, who regard the securing for themselves of another girl's lover a perfectly legitimate operation.

Not infrequently one hears it said that So-and-So is one of the most attractive girls in town, because she can cut any girl out that she tries to. You may say that a man so easily won is no great loss, or that such things may occur in other circles of society but not in yours. Possibly they do not. One does not deny the honor of honorable men and women in any walk in life. But in polite society, fashionable society, these things occur. Oftener in New York than in Boston, and oftener in London and Paris than in New York. Indeed, we may sneer, as we often do, at the primitive customs of the lowly, and at their absurd phrase of "keeping company." It makes a delightful jest. But beneath it is a greater regard for the rights of a man or woman in love than one is apt to find higher in the social scale.

With them, to select one another "to keep company," is like an offer of marriage. To "keep steady company" is the formal announcement of an engagement, which is a potential marriage. It is the first step towards matrimony, and is almost as sacred and final.

With their more fortunate and envied sisters in the smart set, an engagement is the loosest kind of a bond, and neither man nor woman is safe from the wooing of other men and women until the marriage vows have been pronounced, and, if your society is very fashionable, not even then.

So that this society of which I speak would undeniably be called "good."

Now, of course, all women desire to be loved. She is a very queer woman who would deny that proposition if asked by the right person, and I hope he would have sense enough not to believe her if she did. I do not object to a girl making herself attractive to men in a modest and maidenly way. On the contrary, I heartily approve of it. But I would have her select a man who belonged to no other girl, and to know that nothing but misery can result from the taking of a lover away from her friend.

It is the fashion for women to deny that this is done. I never could see why. But possibly they deny it because they are afraid, if they discuss it, that people will think some girl has lured a lover or two away from *them*.

People who have witnessed the outward results of this phenomenon also deny the true cause, on the ground that the robber girl was not clever enough to have done it. That she simply was more to the man's taste than the first girl, and so it was all the fault of the man.

Of course, I cannot deny the fickleness of man. But I do say that the girl hardly lives, no matter how pretty she is, who has not the wit to get another girl's lover if she wants him. It makes no difference how young she is, she never makes the mistake of disparaging the first girl. No woman of the world is less liable to such an error than a girl who deliberately intends to get another girl's lover.

She begins by gaining her confidence. Very likely she manages to stay all night with her. (That is the time when you tell everything you know, just because it is dark, and then spend the rest of your life wishing you hadn't.)

Then, when she has the points of the compass, so to speak, she says she will help her dear friend, and the dear friend, not being clever (or she wouldn't have confided), thinks she is the loveliest girl in the world, and, after promising to send her lover to call in order to be "helped," she calmly goes to sleep, just as if she has not seen the beginning of the end.

The other girl has observed - and she is, of course, pretty and attractive. Girls who do not know anything and who never study are always pretty. It is only the plain girl who is obliged to be clever. The first time she sees the lover of her dear friend she begins to laud her to the sky. She herself is looking so pretty, and she shows off in the most favorable light, while all the time singing her dear friend's praise with such fatal persistency that she fairly makes him sick of the sound of her name and of her namby-pamby virtues. Now the man would hardly be human if he did not tell this artless little creature that he had had enough of her dear friend, and that he would much prefer to talk about herself. Pouts of hurt surprise. She "thought you were such a friend of hers!" She "only wanted to entertain you by the only subject" she "thought would interest you." Presto! The entering wedge! She knows it, but the man does not. He has no idea of being disloyal to his sweetheart, but he is a lost man nevertheless - lost to the first girl and won by the second. Won in a perfectly harmless and legitimate way too. Won while doing her duty, keeping her promise, helping her friend. Her conscience acquits her. She has only observed and made use of her cleverness to know that too smooth and easy a course to true love generally gives him to the other girl.

But in reality she has stolen him - she has committed a real theft. And, personally, I should prefer to know her had she stolen money. You can jail a man who steals your watch, but the girl who steals a man's heart away from his sweetheart walks free, and uncondemned even - to their shame be it spoken - by those who know what she has done.

Nobody dares condemn her - even the friends of the robbed girl, for that presupposes some lack in her charm, and gives publicity to her loss. The wronged girl, because of her pride and conventionality and civilization, makes no outcry. A barbarian in her place would have fallen on the robber girl in a fury and scratched her eyes out. Sometimes I am sorry that our barbaric days are over.

Some of the greatest tragedies in life have come from this disloyalty among girls in their relations with each other.

I have no patience with those people who fall in love with forbidden property and give as their excuse, "I couldn't help it." Such culpable weakness is more dangerous to society than real wickedness.

Love is not a matter of infatuation. It is not the temptation which is wrong. It is the deliberate following it up, simply because the temptation is agreeable. Of course, it is agreeable! You are not often irresistibly tempted to go and have your teeth filled!

Men never will have done with their strictures on girls until girls achieve two things. One is to observe more honor in their relations with each other, and the other is to learn to think.

Lilian Bell

ON THE SUBJECT OF HUSBANDS

"All that I am, my mother made me"

Perhaps you think that girls do not know enough about other girls' husbands to discuss them with any profit. But if there has been a dinner or theatre party within our memory where the married girls did not take the bachelors and leave their husbands for us, we would just like to know when it was, that's all.

I dare say it never occurred to these wives what an opportunity this custom gives us to study social problems at close range. We girls are supposed to be blind and deaf and dumb; but we are none of the three. We try to see all there is to see, and hear all there is to hear, and then, when we get together, we wouldn't be human if we didn't talk it over and tell each other how infinitely better *we* could manage Jessie's husband than she does, and that it seems a pity that Carrie doesn't understand George.

I suppose it would be rather handsome of us always to pretend that we did not hear the covert rebuke or the open sarcasm bandied about between these husbands and wives. On the whole, I think it *would* be chivalrous for us to be utterly oblivious, and talk about the weather, if anybody asked us if we knew that Mary never could spend a cent without having John ask her what she did with it.

That is the way men do when they do not wish to tell on each other. I think men are fine in that way. We girls all think so, only we seldom have the moral courage to emulate their admirable example. We are so fond of "talking things over." And if the married women do not wish us to talk their husbands over, just let them give us our own rightful property, the bachelors, and we will never utter another cheep.

However, I would not give up my small experience with other girls' husbands for a great deal. It has convinced me of something of which I always have been reasonably sure, and that is that American men make the best husbands in the world, and that women who cannot get along with Americans, and who think men of another race, who have more polish, more finesse, more veneer, would suit them better, could not manage to live happily with the Angel Gabriel.

Dear me! If these dissatisfied American wives could only realize that an all-wise Providence had, in the American man, given us the best article in the market, and that when we rebel at our lot we are simply proving that we do not deserve our good fortune, they would never even discuss the subject of having men of any other nationality.

Of course, in every nation there is a class of men who are as noble, as high-minded, as chivalrous as even the most captious American girl could wish. But I refer to the general run of men when I say that there is something about men born outside of America, a native selfishness or callousness, a lack of perception and appreciation of the fineness of womanhood, amounting to a sort of mental brutality, which wellnigh unfits them for close social contact with the super-sensitive American woman. And just as surely as American women persist in disregarding this subtle yet unmistakable truth, just so surely will they lay themselves open to these soul-bruises from foreign husbands which American men, as a race, are incapable of inflicting. I say they are incapable of inflicting them, because American men, in the face of everything said and written to the contrary, are, in regard to women, the finest-grained race of men in the world.

Now in this generalizing, I beg that you will not accuse me of asserting that these strictures are true of every man who is not an American, or that all American men are perfect. But I do wish to state clearly and frankly my admiration for American men as a race. When an American man *is* a gentleman, he is to my mind the most perfect gentleman that any race can produce, because *his* good manners spring from his heart, and there are a few of us old-fashioned enough to plead that politeness should go deeper than the skin.

Now if the assertion is made that the American man makes the best husband in the world, let him not think that there is no room for improvement, for with him it is much the same as it is with the wild strawberry. At first blush one would say that there could be no more delicious flavor than that of the wild strawberry. Yet everybody knows what the skilled gardeners have made of it in the form of the cultivated fruit. Nevertheless, the crude article, found growing wild upon its native heath, is much to be preferred to the candied ginger of other nations.

After admitting that the wild strawberry is capable of cultivation, and even attaining, under skilful care, the highest type of perfection, let no one make the mistake of thinking that the time for such improvement is after they have been grown and placed upon the market. If they are found to be knotty, half green, or in a state of decadence, and you are bound to buy strawberries, you can take them, and, by your native woman's wit, you can dress them into a state of palatableness, even if you have to reduce them to a pulp in the sacred mysteries of a short-cake.

But in order to take all the comfort which strawberries are capable of giving to mankind, they should be perfect in themselves when they come from the hand of the gardener - just as it was his mother's duty to have trained that husband of yours before he came under your influence.

It really is asking too much of a woman to expect her to bring up a husband and her children too. She vainly imagines, when she marries this piece of perfection, with whom she is so blindly in love, that he is already trained, or, rather, that he is the one human being in the world who has been perfect from infancy, and who never needed training. She never dreams of the curious fact that mothers always train their daughters to make good wives, yet rarely ever think of training their boys to make good husbands.

Therefore, unless, like Topsy, they have "just growed" good and kind and considerate, a woman has a life-work before her in training her own husband.

But the fact of the matter is that while we girls receive specific training, to the express end of making good wives, the boys of the family receive only general training of chivalry and courtesy towards all women - not with a view of having to spend the greater part of their lives with one woman, or the tact with which this one woman must be treated.

I wonder what would happen if somebody should open a Select Kindergarten for Embryo Husbands? Yet we girls have been in a similar institution for embryo wives since childhood. We are told in our early teens: "Well, only your mother would bear that. No husband would;" or, "You will have to be more gentle and unselfish with your brother, if you want to make some man a good wife."

A good wife! It has a magic sound!

Of course, every girl expects to marry, and the shadowy idea of making a *good* wife to this mysterious but delightfully interesting personage, who is growing up somewhere in the world, and waiting for her, even as she is waiting for him, makes the hard task of self-discipline easier, for we all wish to make "a *good* wife."

Nor are we taught alone to be gentle and sweet and faithful. We girls have to learn that all-potent factor in a happy life - tact. We are early taught that it is not enough to master the fundamental principles which govern the genus man. We have to discover that each man must be treated differently. We must cater to individual tastes. We must learn individual needs, and fill them. In short, we are taught to observe men, to study them, and then to hold ourselves accordingly.

Pray do not imagine that all this is put into words, or

that we have certain hours for studying how to make good wives, or that it is as rigid or exhausting as a broom drill. It is the intangible, esoteric philosophy which permeates the households of thousands of American families, where the mothers are the companions and confidantes of the daughters. It is an understood thing. You would be surprised to know how young some girls are when they have thoroughly mastered this wonderful tact with men. And what is it that makes the American girl so dangerous for all the other women in the world to compete with? It is because she studies her man. And how did she learn it? By seeing her mother manage her father - or, perhaps, by seeing how easily her father could be managed, if her mother only understood him better.

There is a good deal of progressive thought among girls in this generation.

Why in the world mothers train their girls and boys alike up to a certain point in general courtesy and consideration for each other, and then go on with the girls, teaching them the gentle, faithful finesse which every wife has to understand, yet leaves her boy to "gang his ain gait" just at the formative period of his life, I am not able to say.

If I could only hear some mother say to her son, "Don't let your slate-pencil squeak so! Try not to make distracting noises. You may have a nervous wife, and you might just as well learn to be quiet. There is no sense in thinking just because you are a boy that you can make unnecessary and superfluous noises!" I think I should die of joy! Or how would it sound to hear her say, "Whenever you come in and find your sister irritable, don't simply take yourself out of her way.

Look around and do something kind for her. Make a point of knowing what she likes and of doing it. Life is so much more monotonous for women than for men, you should be especially generous with your sister, so that some day you will make some sweet girl a good husband."

Can't you just *see* what kind of a husband that boy would make?

Romance comes later to a boy than to a girl, but it hits him just as hard when it does come, and a boy is quite as responsive as a girl to the suggestion of a personal chivalry which shall prepare him to be a better husband to a shadowy personality which he cannot do better than to keep in his mind and heart.

Why does a woman, who finds it difficult, perhaps even impossible, to persuade her husband to do certain essential things, never take pity on the poor little girl across the street, who, in ten or fifteen years, is going to marry her son?

Take, at random, the subject of a wife's having an allowance. Thousands of wives have it, and therefore they are not the ones we are to consider. But where there are thousands who possess an allowance from their husbands, or who have money in their own right, there are millions who never have a cent they are not obliged to ask their husbands for.

There is no question of gift about it. At the altar he endowed her with all his worldly goods, and he thinks he has lived up to the letter of his vow when he tells her that all he has is as much hers as his. But unless that oft-quoted saying is followed up by a certain sum, no matter how small, which is in truth her very own, she feels that that clause in the marriage service might as well be stricken out.

When wives as universally share in adding to the general prosperity of the home - by managing the house, keeping their husband's clothes in order, and caring for the children - as men always admit is the case, wives are actually adding dollars to their husband's income. Then ought not a man to divide that same income with her in the form of an allowance, for which, if only to add to her self-respect, he has no more right to call her to account than she has to insist on seeing a list of his expenditures?

I have nothing to say about extravagant or untrustworthy wives, who do not come into the subject at all. I am only referring to the magnificent multitude of good, careful, thrifty, typical American wives, whose sole aim in life is to make a happy home for husband and children. Nor am I denying that these women have all their wishes granted, and are allowed to spend their husbands' money with reasonable freedom, provided they account for it afterwards. I am only asserting that every married woman, from the farmer's wife to that of the bank president, should have some money regularly which is sacredly her own.

Perhaps men think I am exaggerating the evil. Perhaps they do not know that the only advice married women give to engaged girls which *never* varies is: "Be sure you ask for an allowance from the first, because, if you don't, you may never get it."

I suppose that the majority of men do not know that their wives hate to ask them for money. Of course it does not seem so terrible to those of us whose fathers occasionally want to keep back enough money to buy coal when our daughterly demands get refused. But it never occurs to us that a girl's lover-husband, this courteous stranger whom she has loved and married, would ever forget his theatre and American-Beauty days sufficiently to say: "What did you do with that dollar I gave you yesterday?"

Now, frankly speaking, it never occurs to unmarried girls that the honeymoon can ever wear off. We look upon husbands as only married sweethearts. We sort of halfway believe them - at least we used to, before we observed other girls' husbands - when they tell us that they long for the time when they can pay our bills and buy clothes for us. We never thought, until we were told, that any little generous arrangement, which we expected to last, must be fixed during the first few weeks of marriage. I dare say most of us had planned to say, in answer to the money question, "Just as you like, dear. I'd rather have you manage such matters for me. You know so much more about them than I do." It is a horrible shock, from a sentimental point of view, to be told to say, "I'll take an allowance, please," and then, if two amounts are mentioned, to grab for the biggest. Oh, it is a shame! It is a shame to be told that we shall be sorry if we don't, and to know that we shall have no opportunity to show how unselfish and trusting we are.

It is all your fault, you men, that you do not think of these things more. You might stop a moment to consider that it *is* rather a delicate matter for a woman to ask money of a man. If your wife is like most wives, she is doing as much to help you make your money as you are. She is keeping you well and happy and your home beautiful. You could not keep your mind on business an hour if she did not. Therefore she deserves every dollar which, after discussing your future life together, you feel that you can afford to give her. She ought to be made to feel that she has earned it, and that she may spend it freely and happily, or invest it, just as she chooses. Do you think that you would not get the whole of it back if you were ill and needed it? It is an ungracious thing to call her to account for every dollar. How do you know but that she wants to save a little out of the market-money to buy you a nicer birthday present than usual?

American men are the most lavish husbands in the world. It is only that they do not think what a joy it is to a woman to have even the smallest amount of money of her very own, concerning which no one on earth has a right to question her.

And yet, what is the use of trying to train a husband into a habit of thought like this, when he has been used to hearing his mother *argue* his father into giving her money, and yet to know that she and all the world considered him generous, and that, in truth, he was?

A woman who suffers heartache because her husband never apologizes to her, or who endures mortification unspeakable because she has not a penny of her own, has no right to rebel, even in her own heart, unless she is training her son to make the sort of husband for some little girl, now in pinafores, which she would have wished for herself.

A FEW MEN WHO BORE US

THE SELF-MADE MAN

Somebody has cleverly defined a bore as "a man who talks so much about himself that I never can get a chance to talk about myself." But that is too narrow. I am broad-minded. I want somebody to find a definition large enough (if possible) to include all the bores. I do not know, however, but that I am asking too much.

Neither is this definition entirely true. For I have heard men talk about themselves for hours at a time, and they talked so well and kept their Ego so carefully hidden that I was enchanted, and never mentioned myself, even when they paused for breath. Then, too, I have been bored to the verge of suicide by some worthy soul who insisted upon talking to me of (presumably) my pet subject - myself - and who was doing his poor little best to say nice things and to be entertaining.

A bore is a man or a woman who never knows How or When. There are times in the lives of all of us when it bores us to be talked to of home or friends or wife or husband or mother or religion. There are times when nothing but a large, comfortable silence can soothe the worry and fret of a trying day. At such times let the tactless woman and the thoughtless man beware, because everything they say will be a bore.

It is not wilful cruelty which makes us say that (to a woman) the word "bore" is in the masculine gender and objective case, object of our deepest detestation. Men are oftener bores than women, for two reasons: One is that they seldom stop to think that they could be a bore to anybody; and the second is that we women never let them see that we are being bored, for it is our aim in life to look pleasant and to keep the men's vanity done up in pink cotton, no matter if we are secretly almost dropping from our chairs with weariness - the utter, unspeakable weariness of the soul, compared to which weariness of the body is a luxury.

Women are too tender-hearted. A woman cannot bear to hurt a man's feelings by letting him know that he is killing her by his stupidity. And even if she did, in the noble spirit of altruism, rather than selfishness, the next woman, with one reproachful glance at her, would pick up the mutilated remains of the man's vanity and apply the splints of her respectful attention and the balm of her admiration, partly to add a new scalp to her belt, and partly to show off the unamiability of her sister woman.

So it is of no use to kick against the pricks. Bores are in this world for a purpose - to chasten the proud spirit of women, who otherwise might become too indolent and ease-loving to be of any use - and they are here to stay. We have no conscience concerning women bores. We escape from them ruthlessly. And, perhaps, because women are quicker to take a hint is the reason there are fewer of them. It is only the men who are left helpless in their ignorance, because no woman has the courage to tell them.

Our only defence is in telling the men in bulk what we have not the courage nor the wish to tell the individual, and letting them sit down and think hard, applying the relentless microscope of self-analysis to their carefully tended Ego, to see if, haply, any of these things we say apply to themselves.

Of course, this is hard on men, because very likely some of those who have been led by women to believe that they are entertaining, even to the verge of fascination, are the very ones who are the greatest bores. But we women do our best. We are hampered by our supposed amiability, and bound up by a thousand invisible cords of tact and policy to a line of action which dupes the cleverest of men. And we are shrewd enough to know that if we should become what they now, in the smart of their wounded vanity, would call honest, they would simply turn their broadcloth backs upon our uncalled-for frankness and seek the honeyed society of some sweet woman who flattered them exactly as we used to flatter them before we became so "honest."

Ah, well-a-day! Enter the self-made man. And with him the commercial spirit of the age. Enter the clink of coin and the unctuous corpulence of a roll of bills. Enter the essence of self-satisfaction, the glorious spectacle of a man who spells "myself" with a capital M.

Have you never noticed the change in conversation with the entrance of a new person? How, when a lovely girl enters, the men all straighten their ties and the women moisten their lips? How, when the new person is a self-made man, with his newness so apparent that he seems to exhale the odor of varnish and gilt - how all repose vanishes, and whatever of crudity there is anywhere suddenly makes itself known, and rushes forth to meet the wave of self-boasting which sweeps all before it when the self-made man speaks?

And yet I approve of the self-made man in the abstract. It is the true spirit of Americanism which caused him to raise himself from the ranks of the poor and obscure, and educate himself, or, more likely still, grow rich without education. But is it necessary for him to have the bad taste to boast of it, and never let you forget for one moment that he is the product of man's hand and that the Creator only acted in the capacity of sponsor?

I admire the pluck, the perseverance, the indomitable energy, the ambition which produced the man of prominence from the raw boy; but, kind Heaven, let us forget for one brief moment, if we can, that he did this thing.

It is not the fact that he is a self-made man that bores us - we honor him for that. But it is his vain boasting - the tactless forcing of his unwelcome personality into general conversation, his weak vanity, which demands our admiration for the toil and hardships he has under-gone, which, if they had served the purpose they should have done, would have made him too strong a man, and too much of a man, to force either pity or admiration from people when it was not freely offered.

The favorite gibe of the self-made man is directed against the college graduate. Let there be a young fellow present who is fresh from college, and let him mention any subject connected with college life, from honors to athletics, and then, if you are hostess, sit still and let the icy waves of misery creep over your sensitive soul, for this is the opportunity of his life to the self-made man. Hear him tear colleges limb from limb, and cite all the failures of which he ever has known to be those of college men. Hear him tell of the futile efforts of college boys to get into business. Hear him drag in all the evidences of shattered constitutions, ruined by study, and then hold your breath; for all this is but preliminary to the telling of the story of a colossal success - the history of the self-made man. You might as well lean back and let him have his say, for he has only been waiting all this time for an opening in the conversation to insert the wedge of his Ego.

It seems to be the prerogative of some self-made men not only to boast of themselves, their wives, their sons, their daughters, their houses, their horses - everything! - but to decry all methods of achievement not their own, and all successes not won by their methods. These are the self-made men who bring into disrepute all the grandeur and glorious achievement of their kind. Why must they spoil it? I implore them to assume a virtue if they have it not. I beg them, with all their getting, to get understanding. And if they will not open their eyes and see the anguish they are causing, if they cannot detect the fixed smile of polite endurance on the tired faces of their patient women friends, there will come a day, and we can already see its faint glimmering in the East, when we shall not care whether they are self-made, and we could even live through it if they were not made at all.

THE DYSPEPTIC

The dyspeptic generally wants to tell you all about it. That is a bore to begin with; for nobody in the world wants to hear anybody in the world tell all about anything in the world. Oh, those wearisome, breathless people, who insist upon giving you the tiresome details of insipid trivialities! There is no escape from them; they are everywhere. They are to be found on farms, in mining-camps, in women's clubs, in churches, jails, and lunatic asylums, and the nearest approach to a release from them is to be fashionable, for in society nobody ever is allowed to finish a sentence.

This sort of a bore can only be explained on the microbe theory. None other can account for its universality. You can carry contagion of it in your clothes and inoculate a person of weak mental constitution, who is of a build to take anything, until, in a fortnight, he or she will be a hopeless slave to the tell-all-about-everything habit. There is nothing like the pleasing swiftness of some of our modern diseases about it - such as heart failure, which nips you off painlessly. It is rather like the old-fashioned New England consumption, which gives you a hectic flush and an irritating hack, but which you can thrive on for fifty years and then die of something else.

I never heard of a yacht which did not carry at least

one of this particular breed of bores upon every trip. I never heard of a private-car party which was free from it. Or, if you do not carry them with you, you meet them on the way, and they ruin the sunset for the whole party.

Something ought to be done about it. There ought to be a poll-tax on bores. Mothers ought to train their children to avoid lying and boring people with equal earnestness. Infirmaries should be established for the purpose of making the stupid interesting, or classes organized on "How to be Brief," or on "The Art of Relating Salient Points," or on "The Best Method of Skipping the Unessentials in Conversation." *I* would go, for one.

I quite envy a man who is an acknowledged bore. He is so free from responsibility. *He* does not care that the conversation dies every time he shows his face. He is used to it. It is nothing to him that clever men and women ache audibly in his presence. *He* has no reputation to lose. The hostess is not a friend of his, for whom he feels that he must exert himself. A bore *has* no friends. He is a social leech.

It implies, first of all, a superb conceit to think anybody wishes one to tell all about anything, but conceit is a natural attribute - a twin brother of its sister, vanity - and everybody has it to a greater or less degree. Indeed, the cleverest man I know - quite the cleverest - is one who always panders to this particular foible because he recognizes its universality. He has a country-house, which is always full of guests, with a great many girls among them. Every afternoon, when he drives out from town, his first sentence is, "Now come, children, and tell me all about everything. Who has been here, and what they said, and what you thought, and everything that has happened, including all that is going to happen. Don't skip a word."

See the base flattery of that! Is it any wonder that his house is always full? What bores he would be responsible for making if we were stupid enough to do as he asks! The chief reason people do not is that ten people cannot tell all they know about everything, even if they want to. He is only furnished with two ears.

The dyspeptic is one who makes the most valiant effort to try. His dyspepsia is the most important issue of the world with him, and he *will* talk about it. He cannot keep still and let other people enjoy their sound digestion and healthful sleep. He will not even let other people eat in peace. When he refuses a dish at table he must needs tell you why - just as if you cared!

"Have some coffee, Mr. Bore?"

"No, I thank you, Madame Sans-Gene. I like coffee, but it doesn't like me!"

Irritating, maddeningly reiterated words - the trademark of the dyspeptic bore! I feel like saying, "I agree with the coffee. *I* don't like you either!"

A dyspeptic disagrees with me as religiously as if I had eaten him.

No wonder a man is ill who never thinks or talks of anything but the seat of his ailment, for talk about it he will, and tell you that he cannot eat hot breads or pastry or griddle-cakes or waffles. And if any of those adorable things which your soul loves are on the table, he will sit and watch you eat them, with his hand on his own pulse, and will entertain you with cheerful statements of how he would be feeling if *he* were eating any of the deadly poisons, until it nearly gives you indigestion to hear him describe it.

I dare say I know plenty of women dyspeptics, as long as dyspepsia is said to be our national ailment, but if I do I never hear them talk about it.

Of course every woman knows that a sick man is sicker than a thousand sick women, each of whom is twice as sick as he is. We all know that he can groan louder and roll his eyes higher and keep more people flying about, and all this with just a plain pain, than his wife would do with seven fatal ailments. Then to hear him tell about it, after he has recovered, is to imagine that he is Lazarus over again, and that the day of miracles has returned, that he ever lived to tell the tale. All this refers to an acute attack. But when his trouble is chronic, and it has to do, like dyspepsia, with a man's eating! - you cannot escape. He *will* tell you all about it.

In the first place, dyspepsia is such a refined and lady-like trouble. It has no disgusting details. You can refer to it at all times without fear of nauseating your hearers. In the second place, you can count on nearly half of your hearers having it too, as dyspepsia is almost as catching as Christian Science.

Carlyle was the most famous of dyspeptics. But magnificent as he was in his growling, I fancy it is more bearable to read about it than it was for that adorable wife of his to hear him talk about it. How well we can imagine her feelings when she wrote, "The amount of bile that he brings home is awfully grand."

But one forgives much of his dyspeptic talk, and even allows the mantle of one's Christian charity to cover the sins of lesser bile-cursed men to hear how he sums up the subject:

"With stupidity and sound digestion, man may front much. But what, in these dull, unimaginative days, are the terrors of conscience to the diseases of the liver? Not on morality, but on cookery, let us build our stronghold. There, brandishing our frying-pan as censer, let us offer sweet incense to the devil and live at ease on the fat things he has provided for his elect."

I really do feel sorry for dyspeptics when I read a thing like that. I am not heartless. It must be a sad thing not to be able to eat lobster and ice-cream together, and to have to say "No" to broiled mushrooms, and not to dare to eat Welsh-rarebits after the theatre, and to have to lock up your chafing-dish. But I do say this: unless a man can talk of his trouble as cleverly as Carlyle - and some of the choice dyspeptics I know can almost do that - I want them not to talk at all. If they suffer, let them do it in silence. If they die, let them die entertainingly, or else, I say, don't die in public.

I never see a dyspeptic with his little pair of silver scales on the table, weighing out two ounces of meat, or one ounce of bread, and looking like a death's-head at a feast, and talking like a grave-digger with Yorick's skull for a theme, that I do not think of this:

"Fantastic tricks enough man has played in his time; has fancied himself to be most things, even down to an animated heap of glass; but to fancy himself a dead iron balance for weighing pains and pleasures on was reserved for this, his latter era."

THE TOO-ACCURATE MAN

Women often complain that men in society will not return measure for measure in conversation, but stalk about dumb and unanswering, leaving women gasping from the fatigue of entertaining them.

But I am on the side of the men. I always am. They are a misjudged and maligned set. I approve of men keeping silence when they have nothing to say. It shows that they recognize their limitations and refuse to rush in where angels fear to tread.

Is not a wise silence sometimes to be preferred to the wisest speech? Is there not often a finer eloquence in an answering silence than the cleverest words could express?

A man who talks constantly has a thousand ways always at hand in which to make a fool of himself. A silent man has but one, and even then there are always those who insist upon thinking that he is silent because of his wisdom, and not from lack of it, although Eliza Leslie says, "We cannot help thinking that when a head is full of ideas some of them must involuntarily ooze out."

But as a stimulus to conversation, an intelligently silent man is as instantaneous in his effect as music or eating.

Men have become famous as conversationists who only sat and looked admiringly at vivacious women. It is a rare accomplishment, that of wise silence. It is more of a delicate compliment, more condensed and boiled-down flattery, more scent of incense than the most fulsome speech. And if one's victim is rather a voluble talker, with a reputation for wit, a man need never rack his brains beforehand, wondering what to say, or how he can keep up with her. Let him listen to her, with his metaphorical mouth open in wrapt admiration, and she is his.

Silence is a weapon. It is a powerful corrective when used against a silent person, who then sees himself as others see him. It is a defence, used against the indiscreet, and in the hands of wise men it is a suit of armor. Silence is never dangerous, unless, like a gun, in the hands of a fool. How, then, can women complain of silent men, unless they mean fools, and if they do, why not say so, and fortify their drawing-rooms with music-boxes or magic lanterns?

But anything so negatively unhappy as silence is the least of one's bores. One is seldom annoyed by the persistence of a silent man, for silence often means shyness; therefore it is in our power to curtail his usefulness. But, on the other hand, take a type of the talkative man, the literal, too-accurate man, who insists upon finishing his sentences, and who will stop to dot his i's and to cross his t's, and whose dates are of more moment than his soul's salvation - can anything be done for *him*?

"Avoid giving invitations to bores," says a clever woman, "they will come without."

Alas, how true! The too-accurate man is ubiquitous. If you hear of him, and refuse to meet him, it is only to find that he has married your best friend, whom worlds could not bribe you to give up. If you weed him out of your acquaintance, it is only to realize that he was born into your relationship a generation ago, before you could prevent it. Sometimes he is your father, sometimes your brother. Both of these, however, can be lived down. But occasionally you discover that, in a moment of frenzy, you have married him! Heaven help you then, for "marriage stays with one like a murder!"

Imagine living all one's life with a man who relates thus the trivial incident of having walked with a friend up Broadway last Thursday afternoon, when he met two little boys about ten years old who asked him to buy a paper:

"Last week - Thursday, I think it was, though perhaps it was Friday, or, maybe, Saturday. Let me see: when did I leave my office early? It must have been Thursday, because Friday I stayed later than usual. Yes, it *was* Thursday. It was about four o'clock, perhaps a little later - a quarter after four, or maybe half-past, but I hardly think it could have been as late as that. I think it was nearer four than half-past. Anyway, I was walking up Broadway with a man by the name of Bigelow. Bigelow? Bigelow? Was that his name? It commenced with B, and had two syllables. Boswell? Blackwell? Blayney? What *was* that fellow's name? I never can tell a story unless I get the man's name right. Bilton? Bashforth? Buckby? No, not Buckby, but that sounds like it. Buckley? That's it. That was his name! I knew I'd get it. Well, I was walking up Broadway with Buckley, and at about Thirty-fourth Street - Wait a moment - *was* it Thirty-fourth Street? It couldn't have been that far up. About Thirty-second Street, I think. I don't quite remember whether we had passed the Imperial or not. But it was within a block of it, anyway, when we met two little boys about ten years old - perhaps one was a little older; one looked about ten, and the other about eleven, or perhaps even twelve, although I think ten would come nearer to it - and they asked us in a tone between a whine and a cry - the word whimper more nearly describes it - if we would buy either a *Sun* or a *World* - I've forgotten which."

Delectable as honesty is in a bank clerk, or would be in a lawyer, one yearns for a little less accuracy in the moral makeup of the too-accurate man; for a little of the celestial leaven of exaggeration in the dusty dryness of his dead-level garrulousness. What difference does it make whether the Revolutionary War took place before or after the discovery of America, as long as you make your war anecdote interesting? Who cares whether Napoleon or Wellington came out ahead at Waterloo, as long as your listener is kept awake by your recital?

I related a sprightly incident only last night about a watch which Francis the Second gave to Mary Stuart, only with my usual airy touch I said Francis the Second gave it to Marie Antoinette! What difference does it make? They were both Marys, and they are both dead.

A most unpleasant old party corrected me, and added: "Francis died about two hundred years before Marie Antoinette was born."

"Then all the more of a compliment that he should

have given her the watch!" I said. And I fancy I had him there.

That is the sort of man who interrupts his wife's dinner-stories all the way through with, "1812, my dear"; "Ouida, not Emerson"; "Herod, not Homer"; until *I* shouldn't be surprised to see her throw a plate at his head. Oh, isn't it fine that one does not dare to do all the things one feels like doing in society?

There is only one way to get even with the too-accurate man, and that is, when he has finished his most exciting story, to say, "And then what happened next?"

Accuracy is almost fatal to a flow of spirits. If one is obliged to weigh one's words, one may live to be called a worthy old soul, but one will not be in demand at dinner-parties.

The too-accurate man need not pride himself upon his honesty above his fellow-men. Oftenest he is to be found paying lithe of mint, anise, and cumin, and neglecting the weightier matters of the law - justice, mercy, and truth. He strains at a gnat and swallows a camel. He is not more trustworthy than the man whose conversation is embellished with hyperbole, because he at least has the wit to discriminate, and the too-accurate man is only stupid.

In essentials, the man who decorates his conversation with mild but pleasing patterns of that style of statement made famous by one Ananias, is to be depended upon quite as surely as the man who takes all the sunshine from the day, and leads one's thoughts to dwell on high, by spending ten minutes trying to recall whether he dropped that stone on his foot before or after dinner. He, and not your own evil nature, should be responsible for your instinctive wish that he had happened to be toying with a bowlder instead of a small stone which could only mutilate.

The painful accuracy which makes some men such deadly bores is a form of monomania. It is the same sort of trouble which afflicts a kleptomaniac. She will steal the veriest trash, just so she can be stealing. He hoards the most useless trifles until his mind is nothing but a garret filled with isolated bits of rubbish that nobody wants to hear, unless one has an essay to write; and even then it is easier to consult the encyclopaedia.

I never believe a statement made by a too-accurate man one bit more quickly than one made by a genial, entertaining diner-out. If it were on the subject of timetables, just between ourselves, I should take the trouble to verify both.

THE IRRESISTIBLE MAN

To other men, the irresistible man too often means the man who publicly ogles women. That is because men can *see* him. But to women, what we can see forms but a small portion of our lives. We hear more than we see, and feel more than we hear. George Eliot says: "The best of us go about well wadded with stupidity, otherwise we would die of the roar that lies on the other side of silence."

But most men have to see things, and they can always see the ogling man, and he always makes them perfectly furious. Queer, isn't it, when the Simon Tappertits of this life are the least of the men who bore us? In fact, I never should have thought of him if some man had not spoken of him. And while I occasionally have been honored by the exertions of one of these insects to attract my attention, thereby proving that I am a woman, I can honestly say that I never remember seeing one. Women who are capable of being really *bored* never even see such men; any more than if you were being roasted alive you would care if a hairpin pulled.

It is a mistake to confound the irresistible man with the fool. Neither is he stupid. Very often he is a man of no small amount of brain. He is, of course, always conceited, and generally, though not always, handsome. I am not describing the soft, sapient, pretty man who lisps, nor the weak-kneed young gentleman with pink cheeks who sings tenor. Far worse. The irresistible man, as *we* know him, is often a man who is doing a man's work in the world, and doing it well. He is frequently a man of character, but through that character runs this strange, irritating thread of conceit, which blinds our eyes to whatever of real worth may be within, because of his exasperatingly confident exterior.

We should brush him aside as carelessly as if he were a fly should there be nothing to him worth hating. But the maddening part of it to us is that the irresistible man is worth saving, only he will not be saved. He thinks he is perfect as he is. If he could get our point of view and let some woman take a hand at him, she might efface his irresistibleness and make a man of him. But no, the irresistible man is in this world to give points - not take them.

A queer thing about this particular type of the irresistible man is that he nearly always has grown up in a small town and has only come to the city because his village got too small for his talents. That of itself explains his whole attitude towards the world. Having probably been the "show pupil" at school, having taken prizes and ranked first among his fellows until he was twenty-one, he brings that confident attitude with him and plants himself in the heart of the great city, like Ajax defying the lightning, without the thought that changed environments might demand change of conduct as well as change in clothes.

Doubtless the whole town helped to spoil him. Doubtless he has heard all his life that the town was too small for him, and that a man like himself ought to go to the city, where there would be a market for his talents. Doubtless he has conquered the hearts of all the village maidens; therefore he expects the same arts to win among city girls. This system of easy victory and of yearning for other worlds to conquer, instead of making him fit himself capably for a larger field, has, on account of this absurd fault of irresistibleness, only made him superficial. His crudeness is, to the uninitiated, almost pitiful. Having never been obliged to work for pre-eminence, he descries exertion, and never admits that he has to try hard to win anything. His cheap little accomplishments of singing - badly - possibly even of reciting dialect with realistic effects, he is accustomed to say he "just picked up." I often have thought that he must have picked them up after somebody else had thrown them away. But they have been efficacious in his town, and in a larger field, with foemen more worthy of his steel, they are intended to enslave.

The irresistible man is too pitiful to laugh at with any degree of comfort. The pathos of the situation is almost too apparent. That is one reason why he is allowed to go on as he is. It is why no one has the heart to try to correct him. What *can* you say to a man whose confidence in his power to please you is such that at parting he says: "I cannot spare you another evening this week, but I'll come next Thursday if I can. Don't expect me, however, until I let you know, and don't be disappointed if you find that I can't come, after all."

To be sure, you have not asked him to repeat his visit at all. To be sure, you have nearly died during this call which is just over. But what are you going to do? We have a white bulldog whose confident attitude towards the world is quite like that of the irresistible man. Jack blunders in where nobody wants him, and puts his great, heavy paw on our best gowns, and scratches at the door when we want to sleep, and gets under our feet when we are trying to catch a train, and makes a nuisance of himself generally. But he is so sure that we love him that we haven't the heart to turn him out-of-doors. We simply endure him, because he is a dumb brute who is so used to being petted that everybody tolerates him, and nobody tries to improve him or teach him better manners.

Confidence is a beautiful thing. But it is also one of the most delicate of attributes, and requires the daintiest handling. The man who is confident with women must be very sure of a personal magnetism, or of sufficient merit to insure success, otherwise his confidence will prove the flattest of failures. The only difference between the irresistible man who bores us to death and the successful man who is so fascinating that he cannot come too often, is that one has confidence with nothing to base it on, and the other bases his confidence on fact.

Women are not looking for flaws in men. They are only too anxious to make the best of sorry specimens, and shut their eyes to faults, and to coax virtues into prominence. Men have nothing to complain of in the way women in society treat them. They get better than they deserve and much better than they give. So all they will have to do to win a better opinion will be to deserve it, and, if they make never so slight an advance, they will see that they are met more than half-way by even the most captious critics of their acquaintance.

Adaptability is a heaven-sent gift. It is like the straw used in packing china. It not only saves jarring, but it prevents worse disasters, and without it a man is only safe when he is alone. The moment he comes into smart contact with his fellow-beings there is a crash, and the assembled company have a vision of broken fragments of humanity, which might have remained whole and suffered no more injury than a possible nick had the combatants been padded with adaptability. The irresistible man is the man who thinks he can get through the world without it. The irresistible man is the one who is so perfect in his own estimation that he needs no change. He is beyond human help.

THE STUPID MAN

His opposite, the clever man, said to me yesterday: "You know, to be actually interested is as likely to make one grateful as anything in this world, unless it be a realization of the kindness of Fate in sparing us the perpetual society of fools."

The perpetual society of fools! Think of it, and then revel, you women, in the thought that we are only bored occasionally - once a week, say, or once a day, or once every two hours, taking our bores as we do ill-flavored medicine. It never occurred to me before I heard that phrase that life held anything more wearisome than to be bored occasionally.

I have read *Ben-Hur*, and thought how awful it would be to be a galley-slave. I have read *The Seats of the Mighty*, and shuddered at the idea of being imprisoned for five years alone and without a light. I have seen a flock of sheep driven by shouting, panting, racing little boys, and have been glad I did not have to drive sheep for my daily bread. I have rejoiced that my lot was not that of a Paris cab-horse, but I never in all my life thought of any fate so appalling as that contained in those words - the perpetual society of fools.

Why not reform our penitentiary methods? What is a prison cell to a clever embezzler, if he can have books and a pipe? Nothing but a long rest for his worn-out nerves - possibly a grateful change.

But what would be the feelings of a man of brilliant intellect - for the accomplished villain is always clever - who was detected in his crime, and who stood breathless before his accusers, waiting for and expecting a life sentence at hard labor, to hear the judge's voice pronounce sentence, "Condemned for life to the perpetual society of fools!"

I believe the man would be taken from the court-room a raving maniac.

I cannot but think that a real fool is conscious of his own foolishness. He must realize his aloofness from the rest of mankind, and in moments of such bitter self-knowledge I can picture many whom the world regards as too far gone to comprehend their calamity praying the prayer of the court-jester, "God be merciful to me a fool." I am a little tender towards such. I do not condemn them. They have reached the stage when they are the victims of human pity - a lamentable condition. But those dense persons inhabiting the thickly populated region bordering on foolishness - those self-satisfied, uncomprehending egotists occupying the half-way house between wisdom and folly, known as stupidity - against such my wrath burns fiercely. They are deceptive - so un-get-at-able. They wear the semblance of wisdom, yet it is but a cloak to snare and delude mankind into testing their intelligence. They are not labelled by Heaven, like the fools we may avoid if we will, or to whom we may go in a spirit of philanthropy. They do not wear straw in their hair like maniacs, nor drool like simpletons. Now they infest society clad in the most immaculate of evening clothes.

Often they are college graduates, and get along very well with other men. They are frequently found among the rich, sometimes even among the poor. Sometimes they are stolid and cannot understand. Sometimes they are indifferent and won't understand. Sometimes they are English.

We women are those upon whose souls their stupidity bears most heavily. But stay - they do not oppress all women alike! There are women whose spiritual needs never soar above the alphabet. When these men are men of family, and one expects to find their wives sitting with clinched hands and set teeth, simply enduring life and praying for death, one is often surprised to see that they are generally stout women, who wear many diamonds and a bovine expression in their eyes. Evidently there is no nervous tension in their house, and the dense man is quite capable of comprehending the a b c of human nature and of keeping his family in flannels.

In strictly fashionable society the stupid man is not conspicuous, because one never has time to comprehend that one is not understood. If he nods his head sagely and says nothing, one is probably grateful and passes on to the next, thinking that he is most entertaining. But in that society where one sometimes sits down and breathes, where conversation is considered as a fine art, and where talk is a mutual game of battledoor and shuttlecock, then it is that your stupid man looms up on the horizon like a blanket of clouds.

In America, particularly, conversation is something which not even the French, who approach it most nearly, can thoroughly understand, for with all its blinding nimbleness and kaleidoscopic changes there is a substratum of Puritan morality which holds some things sacred - too sacred even to argue in public - and one who transgresses turns off the colored lights, and lo! your conversation is all in grays and browns. To converse properly in America one must possess not only a nimble wit and a broad understanding, but he must take into consideration one's pedigree, and the effect of the climate.

This practically bars the stupid man from ever hearing the sound of his own voice outside the secluded walls of his own home - or should. It ought also to bar the simply witty man; for what is more jarring than a misplaced wit or an ill-timed jocularity?

No, the chief requisite for a seat among the glorious company of the elect is a deep-seeing, far-reaching, sensitive comprehension; a capacity to see not only through a thing but over it and under it and beyond it; to see not only its derivation and ancestry, but its purport and import and influence and posterity; to detect the inner meaning and the double meaning, and to smile alone at its surface meaning. There are those of us, particularly women, who must have this all-enveloping comprehension if we are to be thought fit to live. Our conversation is such that, if we were taken literally, we deserve to be strangled.

In this day of mad competition in every walk in life, it is not those who can shout the loudest, even in those busy marts where voice reigns supreme, who are going to be heard. No one man can continue to shout the loudest. A momentary audience and a raw throat are the most he can expect. But it is he who can exaggerate the most intelligently and overpaint the most subtly.

That sort of impertinence will attract the eye and ear of the most loudly howling mob. Even the wayfarer gets an inkling from a poster, but it is a man of the widest comprehension who gets the whole truth from the subtlest exaggeration, and he who possesses a sense of humor who realizes its acuteness.

To persons of this ilk the stupid man is a calamity compared to which the loss of fortune and back-door begging would be a luxury.

But of course there are grades of stupidity even among stupid men, and of these the educated stupid man is perhaps the most exhausting, because a woman is constantly led into trying to converse with him, having heard rumors that he is a college man, or that he has written a book on mathematics. If a man is a genuine fool, of course one would merely show him pictures, or play games with him, and so save brain tissue. But with the deceptive halfway man, one is defenceless.

A single instance of a *bona-fide* conversation will serve as a fearful warning to the unwary.

A graduate of a German university, a man who has written three books and has a reputation for always winning his lawsuits, sought me out after a dinner, with the fatal accuracy of a man who has dined to repletion and wishes to be amused.

Possibly because I also had dined and was therefore affable, I endeavored to see if there was any forgotten corner of his mind, any blind alley I hitherto had left unexplored, where I might find mine own and feel at home.

His face was dull, heavy, unemotional, but I said in sprightly tones to coax his lethargy:

"I have made such a delicious discovery to-day. I have found that Carlyle has given the most acute definition of humor I ever read. Isn't that rather surprising, when Carlyle's humor is rather lumbering?"

He thought a moment.

"It is," he said, carefully, with that want of recklessness which should endear him to a stone image.

"Do you know it, or shall I tell you?" I said, with fatal geniality.

Another pause.

"Tell me," he said, heavily, wadding his mind with cotton, for fear some lightness should percolate through it.

"Why, he said that humor was an appreciation of the under side of things. Isn't that delicious?"

I spoke with unctuous satisfaction, for I really expected him to comprehend. He looked at my beaming countenance with grave suspicion, and slowly reddened. He said nothing. I still smiled, but my smile was fast freezing.

"Well?" I said, impatiently.

"You are jesting," he said. "That isn't the real answer."

"Why, yes, it is. Do you mean to say that you

don't understand?"

"You jest so much. I never can tell - " he broke off, helplessly.

"But surely you see that," I urged. "How would *you* define humor?"

"Why, humor is something funny. There's nothing funny about - er - that that Carlyle said."

"Yes, but it's only a very delicate and occult way of exhibiting his acuteness," I said. "Don't you see? An appreciation of the under side of things - the side that does not lie on the surface."

"Are you serious?" he asked, as I leaned back to rest from my toil.

"Perfectly. But I can hardly believe that you are."

"Do you mean to say that you really see anything in that definition?"

"I do," I said, with ominous distinctness.

My manner indicated his stupidity, and he resented it. He grew excited.

"Now, tell me, on your honor, do you really see anything funnier in the under side of that sofa than in the top side?"

I could have screamed with anguish. But, being in company, I only smote my hands together in my impotence and prayed for death.

The tension was relieved by the young son of our hostess in the library just beyond having overheard our conversation. He laid his hand over his mouth and went into such convulsions of silent laughter, all the time writhing and twisting his lean body into such contortions that in watching his extraordinary gymnastics over the head of my unconscious *vis-à-vis*, and wondering if the boy ever could untie himself, I forgot my suffering. I even relaxed my mental strain and forgot the stupid man.

Would I could keep on forgetting him.

THE NEW WOMAN

"You have taught me
To be in love with noble thoughts."

That clever *bon-mot*, "To say 'everybody is talking about him' is a eulogy. To say 'every one is talking about her' is an elegy," is no longer true, more's the pity. More's the pity, I mean, because such a delicious bit deserves a longer life. I could weep over the early death of an epigram with a hearty spirit, which is second only to the grief I feel at a good story spoiled for relation's sake. Cleverness, like beauty, is its own excuse for being, and the first attribute of the new woman is her cleverness. It is the new woman who is responsible for the death of that epigram. But as she did not take an active part in the murder, but was only an accessory after the fact, let us hope that she will escape with as light a sentence as possible from that stern old judge, public opinion, who is not her friend.

The newspapers have ridiculed the new woman to such an extent, and their ridicule is so popular, that it requires an act of physical courage to stand up in her defence and to tell the public that the bloomer girl is not new; that they have had the newspaper creation - like the poor - with them always; that they have passed over the real new woman without a second glance. In other words, to assure them as delicately as possible that they have been barking up the wrong tree.

The first thing which endears the new woman to me personally, more even than her cleverness, is that she has a sense of humor. You may deny that, if you want to. I firmly believe it, but I am not infallible. Thank Heaven that I am not. I abominate those people who are always right. You can't amuse yourself by picking flaws in them. They are so irritatingly conclusive. Now I am never conclusive, and you ought to be glad of it. It makes it so much pleasanter for you to be able to disagree with me logically.

Why have men always possessed an exclusive right to the sense of humor? I believe it is because they live out-of-doors more. Humor is an out-of-door virtue. It requires ozone and the light of the sun. And when the new woman came out-of-doors to live, and mingled with men and newer women, she saw funny things, and her sense of humor began to grow and thrive. The fun of the situation is entirely lost if you stay at home too much.

Now don't let the supersensitive men - who always want women to pursue the perfectly lady-like employment of knitting gray socks - don't let them have a fit right here for fear women have come out-of-doors to stay and are never going in-doors again. Even women, my dear sirs, know enough to go in when it rains. They love a hearth-rug quite as well as a cat does. A cat and a woman always come home to the hearth-rug. But there is very little mental exhilaration in a hearth-rug. Lots of comfort, but little humor. The real excitement of life, at least to a cat, is when in a morning stroll abroad she goes out of her sphere - the hearth-rug - and meets some feline friend to whom she extends a claw, playful or otherwise; or possibly meets some merry puppy which induces her to move rapidly up the nearest tree with an agility which you never would believe the mother of a family could boast if you had not been an eye-witness to the interesting scene. Such an encounter will not induce her to want to stay up a tree. It only makes the safety of the hearth-rug more inviting. Now, if she always remained on the hearth-rug, how could we tell, should the hearth-rug be invaded in the absence of her natural protectors, that she could defend herself? For my part, I am glad to know, when I leave her, that she is not so helpless or so sleepy as she looks. It is a great thing to know that a cat's tree-climbing abilities are not hopelessly dormant. It does not make her purr the less when she is stroked. Her fur is as soft, her ways are as gentle as they ever were, and as she lies there so quietly upon the hearth-rug she looks as though she never had left it. Only once in a while she regards you out of one eye in a companionable way, as who should say, "That's all right. You know I *can* climb a tree when occasion requires."

The dear new woman! I like her. Perhaps she is crude in her newness. Give her time. Perhaps she makes a little too much of her freedom. How do you know what she suffered before she became new? Perhaps she has her faults. Are you perfect?

Of course there is the woman who shrieks on political platforms and neglects her husband, and lets her children grow up like little ruffians; the woman who wears bloomers and bends over her handle-bar like a monkey on a stick; the woman who wants to hold office with men and smoke and talk like men - alas, that there *is* that variety of woman - but she is not new. Pray did you never see her before she wore bloomers? Bloomers are no worse than the sort of clothes she used to wear. Her swagger is no more pronounced now than it used to be in skirts. She has always had bloomer instincts. You don't pretend to declare, do you, that there never were unconventional women, ill-dressed and rowdy women, before the new woman was heard of? That is the great mistake you make. These women are *not* new women. We've always had them. We never, unfortunately, have been without them.

The real new woman is a creature quite different. She is one whom you would wish to know. She is one whom you would invite to your most select dinners. You would be better men if you had more friends like her, and broader-minded women if you dropped a few of those who hand you doughnut recipes over the back fence, and who entertain you with the history of the baby's measles, and how they are managing to meet the payments on their little house. I am not unsympathetic, either, with the measles or the payments, but I prefer the subjects of conversation which a new woman selects. There is more ozone in them.

The new woman whom I mean is silk-lined. She is nearly always pretty. She is always clever. She is always a lady, and she is always good. Perhaps, to the cynical, that combination sounds as if she might not be interesting; but she is. Of course not always. One may have all those gifts, and yet not know how to make use of them for other people's benefit. The gift of being interesting is a distinct one by itself. But the new woman, having fresh and outside interests, is generally able to talk of them delightfully.

The new woman is new only in the sense that she has opened her eyes and has begun to see the value of the simple, common, everyday truths which lie nearest to her. The whole world becomes new to those who suddenly awake to the beauties which they never had thought of before.

Once women taught their daughters housekeeping and sewing from stern principle, and made it neither beautiful nor attractive.

Then house-keeping went out of fashion.

Feather-headed boys married trivial girls, and began to make a home without the first gleam of knowledge as to how the thing should be done. The foolish little wife knew not how to cook or sew. The foolish little husband said he was glad of it. He didn't want his wife to wear herself out in the kitchen. Servants could do such things. So they hired servants more ignorant than themselves, "and the last state of that man was worse than the first." Children came to them. That was the most pitiful part of all. A house may be badly managed and ignorantly cared for, and people do not die of it, or become warped or crippled, but the soul of a child, to say nothing of the helpless little body, can be ruined utterly through the irresponsibility of the criminally ignorant people to whom the poor little thing is sent. Their ignorance is so dense and deep-searching that they never know that they are ignorant. But back of it all there is a reason. A bigoted, senseless, false, and misnamed delicacy. Mothers reared their daughters and sent them to fulfil their mission in life, of being wives and mothers, versed in everything except the two things they were destined to be. It was as if a physician were taught architecture, music, and painting, and then sent out to practise his unskill in medicine upon a helpless humanity.

Then the new woman opened her eyes. She read those sturdy words which are much quoted, but which never can be repeated too often: "The situation which has not its duty, its ideals, was never yet occupied by man. Yes, here, in this poor, miserable, hampered, despicable Actual, wherein thou even now standest, here or nowhere is thy Ideal; work it out therefrom, and working, live, be free. Fool! the Ideal is in thyself; thy condition is but the stuff thou art to shape this same Ideal out of; what matters whether such stuff be of this sort or that, so the form thou give it be heroic, be poetic? Oh, thou that pinest in the imprisonment of the Actual, and criest bitterly to the gods for a kingdom wherein to rule and create, know this of a truth - the thing thou seekest is already with thee, 'here, or nowhere,' couldst thou only see."

It read like book-learning when applied to other women. It read like a revelation when applied to herself. She thought what her mission was. To make a home; to be a good wife; to understand and teach little children. And where do you find the new woman now? In the kindergarten colleges; in university settlements; attending mothers' meetings; teaching ignorant mothers how to understand the tender souls and delicate bodies of the dear little creatures committed to their loving but unwise care. You find them well prepared by a course of study to accept the responsibilities of life when their time comes. Is *that* trivial? Is *that* a subject to sneer at or to jest about? Rather it is the hope of the nation.

Legislation cannot satisfactorily restrict immigration.

Lilian Bell

Laws do not forbid the criminal from marrying and the insane from being born. All the masculine wisdom in the world cannot prevent the State from annually paying millions of dollars for the support of those who are foredoomed through generations of ignorance and crime - crime which too often comes only from ignorance - to fill your jails and asylums. Who is doing anything to remedy? The men. Who is doing anything to *prevent*? The women. The new woman, the sneered at, the ridiculed and abused, caricatured by the cartoonist, derided by the press, is going quietly to work with jail-schools, with free kindergartens in tenement districts, with college settlements, to begin with the care of mothers and children. That is just one of the things the new woman is doing. Is she a poor creature? Is she wearing bloomers? Is she masculine or unwomanly? Rather she possesses attributes almost divine in that she strikes at the very root of the matter, and begins a course of action which, if carried out, will do what all the men in creation can never cure. She will prevent.

The new woman is young. The new woman is oftener a pretty girl than otherwise. They are not poor girls either, who are doing these things. They are not obliged to earn their daily bread. They are the daughters of the rich. They are the travelled, cultured, delicately reared girls. They are such girls as, two generations ago, would have disdained anything but accomplishments, who were only charitable with their money, and who never dreamed of giving their own time to such work. They were girls who considered their education finished when they left school.

I glory in the new woman in that so often she *is* rich and beautiful. It is easy enough to be good if you are plain. In fact, there is nothing else left for a plain woman "*to do*." But take these lovely girls who are tempted by society to idle away their days and waste their lives listening to a flattery which may be but a thing of the moment, and let them have sense to see through its hollowness, and want to be something and do something, and it becomes heroic.

Perhaps it is only a fad. Then Heaven send more fads. If it is the fashion to have a vocation and to educate one's self along these lines which never were heard of a few years ago, then for once fashion has accidentally become noble.

It strikes me rather that the reign of common-sense has begun - that the age of utility has come. When nine out of every ten of the girls you meet in smart society have a distinct vocation of their own; when a girl who only sings or plays or crochets is considered by her sister-women to be a butterfly; when society girls are being trained nurses; when, if you are paying calls upon a fashionable friend, you are quite apt to be told that she is living at Hull House this month; when a girl whose face generally appears in the society column suddenly comes out as the composer of a new song; when a girl who dances best at balls calmly announces that she is taking a course at the university; when everything nowadays is gone into so seriously, the time has come to look the question of the new woman squarely in the face - to put a stop to cheap witticisms at her expense and to give her your honest respect.

The new woman has attacked the problem of how to live. Not how to live for show, not how to veneer successfully, but how to get the most good out of life. She is not simply endeavoring to kill time as she once was. She is trying to live each day for itself. She is not living so much in the to-morrows which never come. Having begun to earn her own money, she is learning the value of her father's - a thing the American father has been trying to teach her for fifty or a hundred years, but she could not learn because she saw it come so easily and she let it go so freely.

A man said to me not long ago, "What has got into the girls? Has it become the fashion to economize? All the nicest girls I know are talking of the value of money and of how much is wasted unthinkingly. Are we poor bachelors to take courage and believe that we can afford one of these beautiful luxuries in wives?"

Alas, it is anything but a hint to take courage; for this heavenly phase of the new woman means that when she has learned that she can support herself, so that in case her riches take wings she need not be forced to drudge at uncongenial employment, or to marry for a home, she will be more particular than ever in the kind of a man she marries. For in fitting herself for marriage she is learning quite as well the kind of husband she ought to have. And she will not be as apt to marry a man on account of his clothes or because he dances divinely as once she might have done.

I do not mean to say that the new woman will not marry. In point of fact she will - if properly urged by the right man. But she will not marry so early, so hurriedly, nor so ill-advisedly as before. And therefore the men whom new women marry will do well to realize the compliment of her choice; for it will mean that, according to her light, he has been weighed in the balance and not found wanting. Of course the other women marry on that principle too. The only difference between the new woman and her sisters is in the amount of her light and the use she makes of it.

It is the man who marries the new woman who is going to get the most out of this life; for even in living there is everything in knowing how. And far from leaving man out of her problem in life, her philosophy is teaching her to look for his possibilities with the same anxiety that she employs in studying her own; that to adapt herself to his individuality need not necessarily imperil her own; that the first element in the forming of this perfect home which it is her ambition to establish is perfect congeniality of spirit between herself and her husband.

It is as if the new woman were striving, by making the best of her present environments, and simply developing her woman nature instead of struggling to usurp man's, to enunciate a philosophy of life which I shall so dignify homely duties and beautify the commonplace that her creed might well be:

"We shall pass through this world but once. If there be any kindness we can show, or any good thing we can do to any fellow-being, let us do it now. Let us not defer nor neglect it, for we shall not pass this way again."

Lilian Bell